W9-BVC-932

JUDAISM

Amulet

Star of
David

Shofar

Kippa

Mezuzah

Yad

Tefillin

Seder plate

Dreidel

DK EYEWITNESS BOOKS

JUDAISM

Written by
DOUGLAS CHARING

Dressed
Torah

DK Publishing

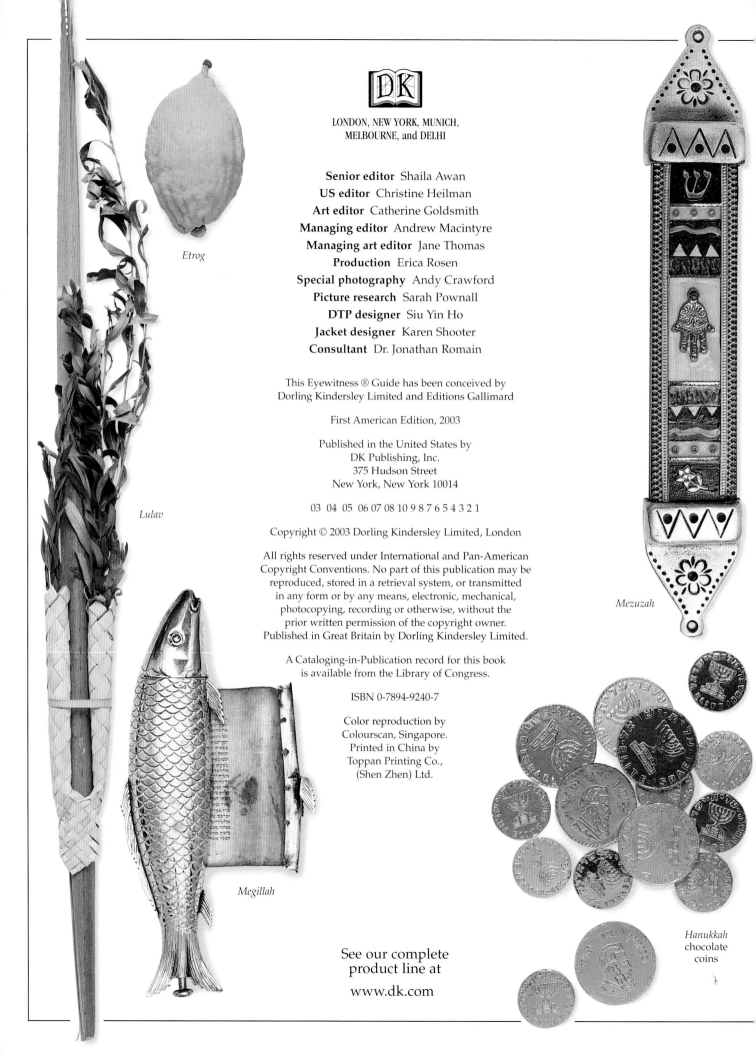

Etrog

Lulav

DK

LONDON, NEW YORK, MUNICH,
MELBOURNE, and DELHI

Senior editor Shaila Awan
US editor Christine Heilman
Art editor Catherine Goldsmith
Managing editor Andrew Macintyre
Managing art editor Jane Thomas
Production Erica Rosen
Special photography Andy Crawford
Picture research Sarah Pownall
DTP designer Siu Yin Ho
Jacket designer Karen Shooter
Consultant Dr. Jonathan Romain

This Eyewitness ® Guide has been conceived by
Dorling Kindersley Limited and Editions Gallimard

First American Edition, 2003

Published in the United States by
DK Publishing, Inc.
375 Hudson Street
New York, New York 10014

03 04 05 06 07 08 10 9 8 7 6 5 4 3 2 1

A Cataloging-in-Publication record for this book
is available from the Library of Congress.

ISBN 0-7894-9240-7

Color reproduction by
Colourscan, Singapore.
Printed in China by
Toppan Printing Co.,
(Shen Zhen) Ltd.

Megillah

Mezuzah

Hanukkah
chocolate
coins

See our complete
product line at

www.dk.com

Contents

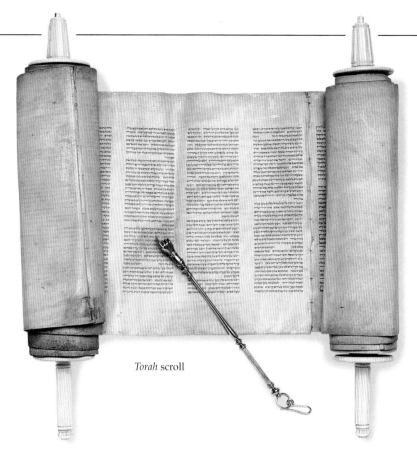

Torah scroll

Being Jewish

KARL MARX

Karl Marx (1818–83) was the founder of communism and is now seen as one of the most important thinkers of the modern world. Although born Jewish, Marx felt nothing for Judaism or any religion. Yet he may have been driven by the teachings of the Hebrew prophets in his work as a social philosopher.

A RELIGIOUS GROUP

To be a Jew is to follow the *Torah* (Jewish scriptures). But even this statement is not simple in today's society. Are Reform Jews more or less religious than Orthodox Jews? Perhaps in their own way, each group can claim to follow the example of Abraham.

THE HISTORY OF JUDAISM reveals a people forced to live in exile. As a result of this, there are Jewish people living in almost every country of the world. However, being Jewish can mean many different things. It can simply describe anyone born to a Jewish woman. This would certainly make someone like Karl Marx Jewish, even though he rejected all forms of religion. For many people, being Jewish means following a religious way of life—embracing their faith all day and every day. Yet there are Jews who do not observe Jewish laws, and rarely, if at all, attend synagogue services. For them, being part of the Jewish people or culture is more important.

"I am a Jew because in every place where suffering weeps the Jew weeps. I am a Jew because at every time when despair cries out, the Jew hopes."

EDMOND FLEG (1874–1963)
Swiss French writer

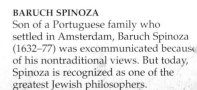

BARUCH SPINOZA

Son of a Portuguese family who settled in Amsterdam, Baruch Spinoza (1632–77) was excommunicated because of his nontraditional views. But today, Spinoza is recognized as one of the greatest Jewish philosophers.

Ultra-Orthodox Jews pray at the Western Wall, Jerusalem

A MUTUAL IDENTITY

The Nazis labeled people Jewish— even those who regarded themselves as being humanist or had converted to Christianity decades earlier. Socialists, atheists (nonbelievers), and ultra-Orthodox Jews were divided in life, but tragically, they shared the same fate because they were all Jews.

Holocaust memorial for the victims of the Dachau concentration camp, Germany

The special day of rest, called Shabbat, *is depicted in this stained-glass window*

This Hebrew text refers to God creating Heaven and Earth and resting on the seventh day

ויכלו השמים והארץ וכל צבאם

Lighting the candles marks the start of Shabbat

Challah *bread (braided loaf) is eaten on* Shabbat

JEWISH CUSTOMS

For some people being Jewish means observing the social customs even if they do not religiously follow the Hebrew Bible. Throughout the year, there are many important Jewish festivals, celebrating key events in the history of Judaism. For some Jews, being part of this rich cultural tradition contributes to their Jewish identity.

A SENSE OF PRIDE

Some religious Jews feel complete with a prayer shawl (*tallit*) over their body and a prayer book (*siddur*) in their hand. But others also identify with fellow Jews throughout the world. They feel a sense of pride when a Jew receives a Nobel Prize or becomes an elected official. Jews also feel proud of the State of Israel—their common home. Some Jews feel it is best to go and live there. Others are rooted in the country they live in, but would like to visit. Their support is for the land and people of Israel rather than specific policies of any one government.

Prayer shawl

Prayer book

How it began

JUDAISM IS ONE OF THE oldest world religions, dating back nearly 4,000 years. It has given birth to two other world religions: Christianity and Islam. At the heart of Judaism lies the belief in one God. Jews can trace their origins and faith to a group of people called Hebrews, later known as the Israelites. These people lived a nomadic lifestyle in a region now referred to as the Middle East. Abraham is seen as the first Jew, and he and his son Isaac and grandson Jacob are known as the patriarchs, or fathers, of Judaism. Jacob's 12 sons were to become the leaders of the 12 tribes of Israel. Their story is told in the Hebrew Bible (Old Testament to Christians).

Clay goblet

Drinking flask

ABRAHAM IS CHOSEN
Although Abraham was born into a society that believed in many gods, as a young man he rejected this form of worship and began to worship one supreme God. Abraham believed that this God was asking him to leave his home in Harran (in what is now Iraq), to become the father of a great nation.

SUMERIAN POTTERY
Archaeological objects such as these provide information about the time in which the stories of the patriarchs are said to have happened. This may have been between 2600 and 1800 BCE (Before the Common Era), with the story of Abraham being the earliest and Joseph's life in Egypt set around 1800 BCE. Excavations of objects help us to understand how people lived and worked in biblical times.

THE COVENANT
The Hebrew Bible tells how God made a covenant (agreement) with Abraham, promising him children who would live in a special land known as Canaan. In return, Abraham and his descendants would have to show God their faith and obedience. This ancient clay column bears the names of Abraham and his descendants.

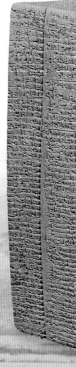

A NOMADIC LIFESTYLE
The Hebrew Bible describes the patriarchs as nomadic people, like the Bedouins today. They lived in large families, or clans, on the edge of the Judean desert, wandering from area to area in search of water and pasture for their animals.

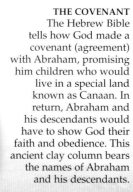

Abraham and the
sacrifice of Isaac

ISAAC
Abraham and his wife
Sarah wondered how
God's promise could
be fulfilled—they were
both very old and could
not have any children.
But Sarah did give birth
to a son, called Isaac, just
as God had promised. To
test Abraham's obedience,
God asked him to sacrifice his
son. Just when Abraham was
about to strike, God told him
to sacrifice a ram instead.
Jewish tradition calls this
story the *Akeda,* which is
Hebrew for "binding,"
because Isaac was only
bound and not sacrificed.

Statue of a
high-ranking
Egyptian
official

THE STORY OF JACOB
Isaac had two sons called
Jacob and Esau. Jacob
was the third and final
patriarch. One night,
God came to Jacob in
a dream and told him
that the land he lay on
would belong to his
descendants. God
renamed Jacob "Israel."
Later, Jacob had 12 sons,
including Joseph, who
were to lead the
12 tribes of Israel.

Detail showing Jacob
and his 12 sons

JOSEPH IN EGYPT
Jacob's favorite son
was Joseph. One day,
his jealous brothers sold
him to some merchants.
Joseph was taken to
Egypt, where he worked
as a slave. The rulers of
Egypt were called
pharaohs. They built
palaces, temples, and
pyramids for their
tombs and treasure.
Joseph managed to
rise to a position of
importance in the
Egyptian court, and
would have dressed like
an Egyptian official.

Bow

Lyre

*Colored
tunics were
made of wool*

*Donkeys were used in
biblical times for carrying
goods and people*

INTO EGYPT
Joseph was reunited with his family when they went to Egypt to
avoid famine in their own land. This Egyptian wall painting is from
the tomb of Khnum-hotep, 19th century BCE. It shows Semitic-looking
people going to Egypt, just as Joseph's family had done with their
herds and goods.

The Promised Land

NEARLY 300 YEARS AFTER Joseph's death, the rulers of Egypt turned against the Israelites. So God chose a man called Moses to lead the Israelites out of Egypt, known as the Exodus, and into the Promised Land of Canaan. The Israelites were given a set of laws to follow, which included the Ten Commandments. After 40 years in the wilderness, they reached Canaan. According to the Bible, it was a land flowing with milk and honey, and was later renamed Israel. It was here that the people would build the Temple and live by the *Torah*. They would have their own kings, priests, and prophets. Above all, God promised them peace and prosperity. In return, they made a promise to God to keep all the laws and to show justice and mercy to the inhabitants of Canaan.

RAMESES II
The Egyptian pharaoh at the time of Moses is thought to have been Rameses II (c. 1279–1213 BCE). Royal records from his court show that he used slave labor to build his cities.

LIFE IN EGYPT
The Israelites were treated harshly by their Egyptian masters. Along with people from other lands, they were used by the pharaohs as slaves, helping to build their cities and temples.

Slaves are depicted making bricks in this Egyptian wall painting

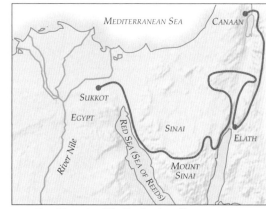

—— *Possible route of the Exodus from Egypt*

THE TEN PLAGUES
As instructed by God, Moses left his home in Sinai and went to Egypt. He asked Pharaoh to set the Israelites free. But Pharaoh refused, so God sent a series of terrible plagues. When the tenth plague struck, every first-born Egyptian boy died, including Pharaoh's son, and so he relented. The Israelites were saved because the angel of death passed over their homes. Led by Moses, the Israelites left Egypt in search of Canaan.

CROSSING THE SEA
It was not long before Pharaoh changed his mind and sent his army after the Israelites, who had set up camp by a sea. It is likely that this was the Sea of Reeds—the original Hebrew translation was the Red Sea, but this was south of the Exodus route. For the terrified Israelites, this was their first test of obedience. They turned to Moses, accusing him of bringing them to harm. But God parted the waters so they could cross safely, and when Pharaoh's army followed, the waters flowed back, drowning the army. The people rejoiced, and once again placed their faith in God to lead them to the Promised Land.

Moses leads his people

The sea closes in on Pharaoh's army

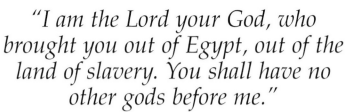

"I am the Lord your God, who brought you out of Egypt, out of the land of slavery. You shall have no other gods before me."

ONE OF THE TEN COMMANDMENTS

GOD'S LAWS

Upon reaching Mount Sinai, Moses received from God the *Torah* (all the laws, including the Ten Commandments). These laws were written on stone tablets and later housed in a special chest, called the Ark of the Covenant. When Moses passed on these laws, the Israelites accepted the covenant of the Lord.

THE PROMISED LAND

When the Israelites approached Canaan, they discovered that the inhabitants could not be defeated easily, and so they rebelled. God condemned the Israelites to wander in the wilderness for 40 years because of their lack of faith. When Canaan was conquered by the next generation of Israelites, the land was divided among the 12 tribes of Israel, who were descendants of Jacob. Pictured above is the Jordan Valley, part of ancient Canaan.

CANAANITE GODS

Canaan was settled by people who worshipped many gods. Baal was one of the most popular Canaanite gods. Such pagan worship was seen as a potential threat to the religion of the Israelites.

Fertility goddess

Bronze figure of Baal

14th-century Bible illustration showing Moses on Mount Sinai

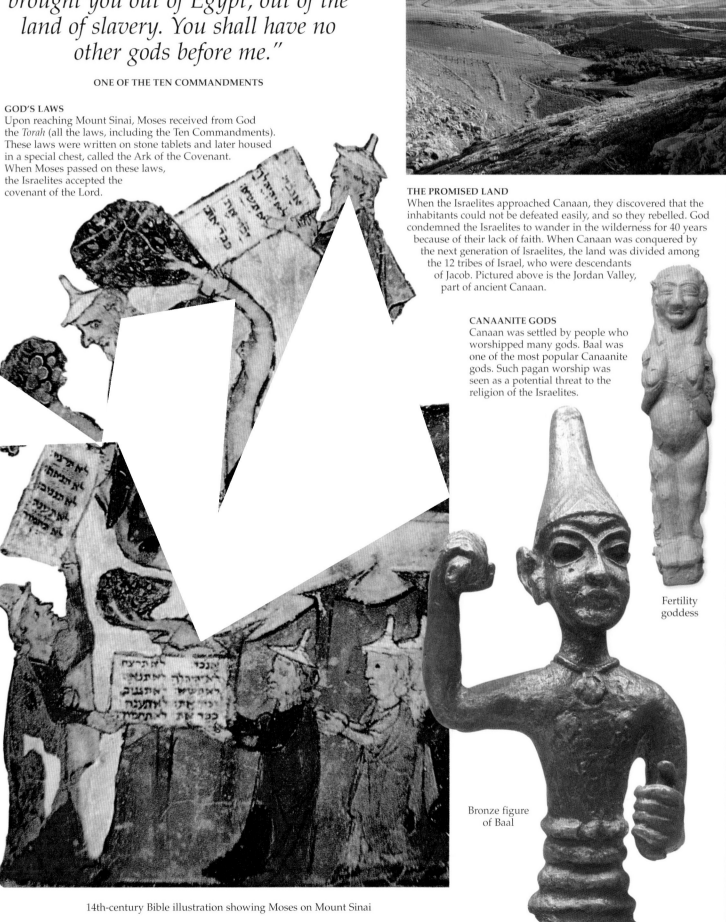

The first kings

SAUL IS ANOINTED
For centuries, the Israelites were led by tribal leaders, known as Judges. They pleaded with the prophet Samuel to ask God to give them a king. Saul, who was known for his bravery, was chosen as the first king to rule and unite the tribes of Israel. During his reign (c. 1025–1004 BCE), Saul organized an army and waged war against many of his enemies. But Saul often disobeyed God. He finally lost his life in battle with the Philistines.

THE RULE OF KINGS in ancient Israel was a gradual process. When the Israelites settled in Canaan, there were many conflicts with the Philistines over land. By the end of the 11th century BCE, the Israelites had been defeated. This led to a call by the people to be ruled by a king, who would unite all the tribes of Israel. Jewish kings were expected to be just and kind, but many were known for their injustice. It was the prophets who criticized both kings and priests when they oppressed the poor and made unjust laws. They also pleaded for moral and religious reform in the country. Often the prophets were regarded as enemies of the state and punished for telling the truth.

THE SEA PEOPLE
The Philistines belonged to a group of people known as the Sea People. From the Aegean area, they sailed to Egypt, finally settling along the coast of Canaan. Findings of Philistine artifacts such as the jug above, dating from the 12th century BCE, indicate a very developed culture.

Jerusalem, from a 15th-century manuscript

"Praise God, all nations, extol the Eternal One, you peoples! For God's love for us is strong, and the truth of God is eternal. Hallelujah!"

PSALM 117

King David's harp may have looked like this musical instrument, called a kinnor

Jerusalem is also known as the City of David

JERUSALEM
Jerusalem had been a Canaanite stronghold until the Jebusites (a group of people from different origins) had taken over the city. When David captured Jerusalem in 1000 BCE, he made the city the capital of his new kingdom, and housed the Ark of the Covenant there. As a result of this, Jerusalem became the political and religious center of the kingdom.

KING DAVID
David, Saul's son-in-law, was the second king of Israel. He reigned for 30 years, joining all the tribes together under one central authority. He also defeated the Philistines. Although he was a warrior king, David is often depicted playing the harp. He is said to be the author of many of the Psalms in the Bible. The Psalms consist of poems or hymns praising God.

THE KINGDOM OF SOLOMON

Solomon, son of David and Bathsheba, was the third king of Israel. His reign was peaceful, and under his leadership the kingdom prospered. Solomon was responsible for constructing many magnificent buildings, including the First Temple in Jerusalem. This provided a focal point of worship for all Israelites, and strengthened the city's religious importance. But soon after Solomon's death in c. 930 BCE, the kingdom was divided between Solomon's son Rehoboam and a military commander named Jeroboam.

This bracelet may have been made from gold stolen by Pharaoh Shishak when he raided the Temple

THE KINGDOM OF JUDAH

In the south was the smaller kingdom of Judah, which was ruled by Rehoboam. The division made Judah vulnerable to attack. The Egyptian Pharaoh Shishak plundered the Temple in Jerusalem, while the Israelites turned to paganism. It was not until the 8th century BCE, under the leadership of King Uzziah (783–42 BCE), that the faith was restored.

Seal belonging to an official in the court of Jeroboam

THE KINGDOM OF ISRAEL

Jeroboam ruled the kingdom of Israel in the north. Israel came into conflict with its neighbors, and it was not until the late 9th century BCE that the kingdom witnessed a more settled and prosperous time. But, like Judah in the south, this prosperity left Israel open to pagan influences.

King Solomon reading the *Torah*, from a medieval manuscript

12th-century detail of Isaiah

THE PROPHETS

The prophets were a group of people who reminded the Israelites of God's ways. They explained what was right and wrong, and did not accept injustice, especially if it came from the king. The prophet Isaiah, for example, protested against those who broke religious law and demanded justice for the poor.

New rulers

JUST AS THE PROPHET AMOS predicted Israel's destruction, the prophet Micah warned of a similar fate for Judah. From the mid-8th century BCE onward, both kingdoms were conquered by a number of foreign rulers. Each new rule brought changes to the way the Israelites lived and worshipped. Under Assyrian and Babylonian rule, the Israelites were exiled and the Temple was destroyed. Nearly 200 years later, a more tolerant Persian ruler enabled the Israelites to return to Jerusalem to rebuild their Temple. But by the end of Greek rule, Judah was plunged into instability, resulting in a short-lived period of independence under the Hasmonean dynasty.

PERSIAN GUARD
King Cyrus the Great of Persia allowed the conquered peoples to follow their customs.

THE ASSYRIANS
By 722 BCE, Israel had been conquered by the Assyrian army. The Assyrian king, Sargon II, deported many of the Israelites to Mesopotamia and in return brought people from his Assyrian empire to Israel. In 701 BCE it was Judah's turn to face the might of the Assyrian army. Lachish, which was southwest of Jerusalem, was destroyed, but Jerusalem was spared.

The entire siege was depicted in stone—this detail shows people fleeing

BABYLONIAN EMPIRE
During the 6th century BCE, a new power emerged—the Babylonians. They invaded Jerusalem in 586 BCE, destroying the city and Temple. As a means of breaking their national identity and preventing them from organizing into rebellious groups, the Israelites were exiled. The clay tablet above records the fall of Jerusalem.

THE REIGN OF KING CYRUS
In the mid-6th century BCE, the Persian dynasty emerged as a powerful force. King Cyrus the Great of Persia conquered Babylon in 539 BCE. He allowed the Jews to return to Jerusalem and rebuild their Temple. Upon their return, the exiled people did not always get along with the Israelites who stayed. Despite the tensions in the Jewish community and the lack of resources, work on the Second Temple began in 516 BCE, led by two prophets, Haggai and Zechariah. In 458 BCE, the prophet Ezra returned with more exiles. He introduced new laws that helped to ensure the survival of Judaism.

A reconstructed model of the Second Temple

Persian silver coin used during this period—on one side is an eagle, on the other side is a lily

THE REBUILDING OF JERUSALEM
In 445 BCE Nehemiah was appointed governor of Judah, and set about rebuilding the walls of Jerusalem. Nehemiah was an important figure in the the Persian court. Not only did he organize the repair of Jerusalem, but he also implemented reforms aimed at strengthening the religion. These included discouraging marriage with non-Jews and prohibiting all work on the Sabbath.

RECAPTURE OF THE TEMPLE
Alexander's early death resulted in a number of conflicts. Judah was eventually conquered by the Seleucids, who ruled over Asia Minor during this period. Heavy taxes were levied, non-Jewish priests were appointed to the Temple, and the people were barred from practicing their religion. The latter led to a revolt in 164 BCE organized by a priest called Mattathias. His son Judah the Maccabee recaptured the Temple and restored the Jewish religion. Today, the victory is still celebrated in the festival of *Hanukkah*.

ALEXANDER THE GREAT
In 332 BCE, Alexander the Great, ruler of Macedonia and Greece, conquered Judah and put an end to Persian rule. He respected the Jewish God and allowed them to run their own affairs. New religious groups emerged at this time, the most notable ones being the Pharisees and the Sadducees. Many Jews accepted Greek culture, called Hellenism, but the Pharisees and the Sadducees did not. The Pharisees observed all Jewish ritual laws and emphasized the importance of the oral *Torah* (the laws given to Moses), while the Sadducees accepted the written *Torah* (the first five books of the Bible).

This bronze coin comes from the reign of Mattathias Antigonus (40–37 BCE)—the last of the Hasmonean kings

Judah the Maccabee stands triumphant

THE HASMONEAN DYNASTY
Judah the Maccabee's victory led to a new line of rulers called the Hasmonean dynasty, which was headed by the Maccabees. But to the dismay of the Pharisees and Sadducees, the Maccabees were influenced by the same Hellenistic culture they rebelled against. Over a period of time, the Hasmoneans started fighting among themselves. Rome, the new emerging power, took advantage of the situation, and ended the Hasmonean dynasty.

Roman rule

Roman bronze helmet, dating from the time when Rome occupied Judea

W HEN THE ROMANS CONQUERED Judea (as Judah came to be known under Roman rule) in 63 BCE, they installed a new ruler, Antipater, whose son Herod the Great later became king of all Judea. The Jews were allowed to practice their faith, but after Herod's rule, a number of Roman policies and the introduction of Hellenistic practices led to several Jewish revolts, all of which were brutally crushed by the Roman army. Many Jews were deported as a form of punishment. This was the start of what is known in Jewish history as the Diaspora (dispersion and was to affect the nature of Judaism.

THE ROMANS IN JUDEA

Herod the Great was given the title "king of all the Jews" in 40 BCE. Although Judea prospered under his rule, the Jewish way of life was greatly threatened. Herod had members of the Hasmonean family put to death because they were seen as rivals. He encouraged foreign influences, and placed a golden eagle (a Roman symbol) on the front of the Temple.

PROCURATORS

From CE 6–66 (Common Era), Rome was ru by a number of officers, called procurator This was a time of considerable unrest, a Jewish rebels, known as zealots, become active. Pontius Pilate (ruled CE 26–36) v the worst of the procurators. He had in of Caesar carried by Roman legions, us the Temple's money for erecting buildi and issued coins with a pagan symbol— curved staff, which was the mark of a R official who predicted the future. This was especially offensive to Jewish people.

Pagan symbol

Coin issued by Pontius Pilate

THE FIRST JEWISH REVOLT

In CE 66, when Jews were celebrating the festival of Passover, Roman soldiers marched into Jerusalem and stripped the Temple of its treasure. The Jews rebelled and succeeded in controlling Jerusalem. But under the direction of Roman general Titus, the rebellion was finally crushed in CE 70. Jerusalem was no longer the focus of Jewish life and faith. The great Roman victory was commemorated in a triumphal arch, which stands in Rome, Italy.

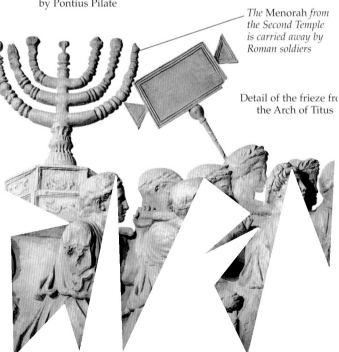

The Menorah from the Second Temple is carried away by Roman soldiers

Detail of the frieze fr the Arch of Titus

Torah scroll

RABBINICAL JUDAISM

Although Jerusalem was destroyed, the faith was given a new direction. Rabbinical schools developed, and the word "rabbi" (master) was used for the *Torah* scholars. With the Temple destroyed, the synagogue became the focus of the faith.

THE BATTLE FOR MASADA

The fall of Jerusalem in CE 70 did not stop the rebels from fighting to the bitter end. Herodium, Machaerus, and Masada were still in the hands of the zealots. Herodium and Machaerus were the first to fall. But Masada was recaptured after a year-long battle. Nearly 960 men, women, and children committed suicide when faced with defeat.

This arrow still had its handle intact

Arrowhead

THE EVIDENCE

Excavations at the fortress of Masada have unearthed a number of objects that would have belonged to the rebels. Among the findings have been prayer shawls, leather sandals, and these arrows, providing evidence of the fighting that took place.

"Masada shall not fall again."

THE OATH TAKEN TODAY BY ISRAELI SOLDIERS

The mountaintop fortress of Masada is located in the Judean desert, overlooking the Dead Sea

KING HADRIAN

Tensions arose once more during the reign of Emperor Hadrian (117–138 BCE). He introduced many changes that angered the Jewish people. Hadrian banned the Jewish practice of circumcision, and embarked upon turning Jerusalem into a Roman city, changing its name to Aelia Capitolina.

Relief of Emperor Hadrian

Coin issued by the Bar Kokhba rebels

THE SECOND JEWISH REVOLT

Emperor Hadrian's policies led to the Bar Kokhba Revolt of 132 BCE. The revolt was led by Simeon bar Kokhba, and was supported by some of the important rabbis of the time, such as Rabbi Akiva. The revolt lasted three years. Thousands of Jewish rebels died, while others were sold into slavery. Jerusalem was now devoid of any Jewish inhabitants, who were forbidden to even enter the city. Just as Jerusalem's name was changed, Hadrian embarked upon changing the name of Judea to Palaestina.

The Middle Ages

15th-century woodcut entitled *Massacre of the Jews*

JEWS OFTEN FACED GREAT religious hostility during the Middle Ages (7th–15th centuries), because Christians blamed Jews for the death of Jesus. This led to hatred and expulsion from Christian countries. England was the first country to expel Jews in the 13th century, followed by France. In Spain and Portugal, attacks against Jews reached a peak in the 15th century. Wherever they lived, Jews had to pay special taxes, were forced to wear certain clothing to single them out, and were often housed in ghettos (segregated areas). Generally, life for Jewish people was better under Muslim rule than it was under Christian rule.

The bell-shaped hat was a mark of disgrace

THE MARK OF DISGRACE
In some countries, Jews were forced to wear clothes with a badge depicting the stone tablets or the Star of David. Some Jews even had to wear pointed hats. All this was done to single them out from Christians and humiliate them.

FALSE ACCUSATIONS
In 1144, Jews in Norwich, England, were accused of murdering a Christian child in order to make unleavened bread (*matzos*) for Passover. This slander came to be known as the Blood Libel, and prevailed for centuries. Jews were also accused of causing the deadly Black Death of 1348 by poisoning wells and rivers. Jews were usually not affected by the Black Death, because they lived in ghettos and maintained higher standards of hygiene, but their good health cast suspicion on them. Many Jews were attacked or murdered.

Muslim soldiers

Crusaders

MONEYLENDING
Jews were not allowed to own land and many other forms of livelihood were closed to them. Since the Church forbade Christians to lend money and charge interest, Jews were forced to become the moneylenders of Europe. Thus a new stereotype emerged: the Jew as a greedy moneylender.

THE CRUSADES
By the 11th century, Muslims had conquered many lands: Syria, Palestine, Egypt, and Spain. Life for Jews living in these countries improved. But by the end of the 11th century, this was to change with the Crusades—a series of holy wars waged by Christians, one of which was to free the Holy Land from Muslim rule. When the first Crusaders left Europe for the Holy Land in 1096, they destroyed the Jewish communities along the way. In 1099, they attacked Jerusalem, killing Jews as well as Muslims.

CHRISTIANITY VERSUS JUDAISM

The Church was a major force in medieval Europe, affecting every aspect of daily life. It held the view that the only hope for Jews and other non-Christians was to convert to Christianity. This supremacy of the Church over Judaism was a popular subject in Christian art at the time. The figure of Synagoga, downcast and holding a broken lance, represented the Jewish faith. The Church, represented by Ecclesia, was always crowned and standing triumphant.

Interior of the synagogue of Toledo—one of 10 synagogues in Spain by the end of the 14th century

The humbled figure of Synagoga

The proud figure of Ecclesia

French manuscript illumination, 13th century

THE "GOLDEN AGE"

Between the 10th and 12th centuries, Jewish communities in Spain and Portugal flourished under Muslim rule. Some cities, such as Granada and Tarragona in Spain, had such a large Jewish population that they came to be known as Jewish cities. A unique Jewish culture developed, giving rise to poets, philosophers, and theologians who coexisted happily with their Islamic and Christian counterparts. But by the end of the 13th century, the status of the Jew changed for the worse. The Christians regained control of Spain, and although tolerant at first, they forced Jews to convert to Christianity or be expelled.

Martin Luther preaching

PROTESTANT REFORMATION

Martin Luther (1483–1546), who led the Protestant Reformation, was at first sympathetic to the plight of Jews. But in later years he preached against them, advocating the burning of synagogues and Jewish schools. Luther also repeated the Blood Libel charges and the poisoning of wells slander.

Life in the Diaspora

Between the 16th and 18th centuries, Jewish communities were founded in a number of European countries, including the Netherlands, Italy, France, England, and Poland. Jews living in these countries enjoyed varying degrees of prosperity and freedom. In Amsterdam, for example, the Jewish community was the richest and largest in Western Europe, and had an enormous impact on the economy. But in Poland, the story was different. There was very little interaction with Polish society, and the majority of Jews earned a meager living—many turning to false messiahs in the hope of salvation. Polish Jews were also denied equal rights, which were granted to Jews of Western Europe.

SHABBETAI ZEVI
Jews believe in the coming of the Messiah, who will pave the way for God's rule. The most famous of the false messiahs was Turkish-born Shabbetai Zevi (1626–76). He became popular with Jews, especially those from Eastern Europe, who were facing great hardship. When he converted to Islam, many of his followers became disillusioned.

SEPHARDI JEWS
Sephardi Jews (descendants of Spanish and Portuguese Jews) first settled in Amsterdam during the 16th century. The Dutch operated a tolerant policy toward Jews, and news of this soon spread. Within a short period of time, large numbers of Jews from Spain and Portugal had moved to the Netherlands. Many of the settlers were educated men—doctors, writers, scientists, and lawyers. Soon, both the Jewish community and the Dutch economy flourished.

18th-century Torah mantle used by Amsterdam's Sephardi Jews

The Ark of the Covenant is woven on the mantle

The crown symbolizes the glory of the Torah

GHETTOS IN ITALY
The policy toward Jews in Italy, which had generally been favorable, changed during the 16th century. The segregation of Jews was made compulsory. In cities such as Venice and Rome, Jews had to live in filthy, overcrowded ghettos, which were a health hazard. Despite this, they were able to follow their faith, and Jewish culture flourished. The picture above shows the Jewish ghetto of Rome, c. 1880s.

Ashkenazi Jews outside their synagogue

ASHKENAZI JEWS
The number of Jews arriving from Eastern Europe (known as Ashkenazi Jews) increased in the 1620s. At first they were dependent on the Sephardi community. Many came from poor backgrounds and lacked the wealth and education of the Sephardi Jews. The artist Rembrandt van Rijn (1606–69), who lived near the Jewish quarter of Amsterdam, took an interest in its life, and often portrayed Jews in his work, as shown above.

MERCHANTS
During the 17th century, Amsterdam became an important center for international trade. As well as being allowed to practice their faith, Jews were allowed to participate freely in economic matters. Merchants were involved with banking, overseas trade, businesses, and with the diamond industry. The latter was to become a Jewish area of expertise—from trading raw diamonds, to cutting and polishing the precious stones.

Diamonds

EQUAL RIGHTS FOR JEWS

By the end of the late 18th century, the granting of equal rights was debated across Europe. In 1789, revolutionary France was the first European country to grant equal rights to Jews. The Netherlands, under the influence of the French Revolution, soon abolished all laws that discriminated against Jews. In other European countries, the call for equality and freedom continued into the 19th century.

Napoleon is shown granting religious freedom

Oliver Cromwell

THE JEWS OF ENGLAND

Jews had been expelled from England since 1290. In 1653 a few Portuguese Jews, who had been forced to convert to Christianity, settled in England. These so-called converts continued to practice their faith secretly. Manasseh Ben-Israel (1604–57), a Sephardi scholar from Amsterdam, petitioned Oliver Cromwell (1599–1658) to readmit Jews. Cromwell, ruler of England after the Civil War, realized that Jews could be of value as they had been for the Dutch economy, and permitted their readmission in 1656. It was not until 1829 that English Jews were granted citizenship.

LIFE IN EASTERN EUROPE

Many of the persecuted Jews fled to Poland during the 1500s. By the mid-1600s, nearly 500,000 Jews lived in this tolerant country. The majority of the inhabitants were poor—peddlers, tailors, and cobblers—living in close-knit communities known as *shtetls*. The synagogue, the rabbi, the *yeshiva* (study-house), and the home were all important features of the *shtetl* community.

Scene from the movie *Fiddler on the Roof*, based on the life of a *shtetl* community

The pogroms

DURING THE 18TH CENTURY, Poland was conquered by three powerful neighbors: Russia, Austria, and Prussia. Its territory was divided among these powers. Nearly all Polish Jews came under Russian rule—which meant over half the world's Jewish population now lived in Russia. These Jews were confined to living in an impoverished area called the Pale of Settlement. Denied freedom of movement, very few options were open to them. The Russian czars (kings) were not sympathetic toward their plight. At first the czars tried to force them to change so that they would follow a Russian way of life. Czar Alexander II (1818–81), however, was more tolerant than his predecessors, and gave hope to Jews. He permitted them to live outside the Pale and lifted some of the legal requirements imposed on them. But his assassination marked a turning point in the history of Russian Jews. It led to attacks on them, known as the pogroms (from the Russian for "devastation"), and thousands of Jews fled in panic.

THE RUSSIAN CZARS
Alexander II reigned from 1855 to 1881. His assassination was blamed on Jews, but it is more likely that he was murdered by his own people. With a new czar—Alexander III (1845–1894)—in place, Jews were once again at the mercy of an unsympathetic ruler. Anti-Jewish attacks broke out; these attacks were both organized and often encouraged by the authorities.

START OF THE POGROMS
The first wave of pogroms (1881–84) resulted in the deaths of hundreds of Jews. Their homes and synagogues were also looted and vandalized, while the police just stood by. In 1882, Alexander III passed the May Laws, which imposed restrictions on Jews. These laws also helped to reinforce the view among many Russians that Jews were responsible for the assassination of the czar. The second wave of pogroms (1903–06) followed a similar pattern of death and destruction.

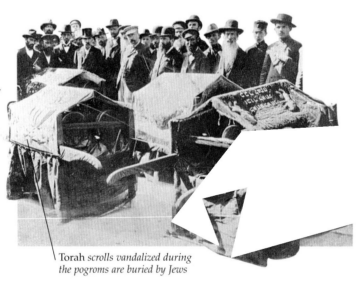

Torah *scrolls vandalized during the pogroms are buried by Jews*

Frightened Jews start to leave Russia

THE JEWISH RESPONSE
There was very little Jews could do to protect themselves during the pogroms. One course of action was to escape from Russia. Others rallied behind the socialists, who wanted to change the way Russia was ruled. Many of the socialist leaders were Jewish, and this fueled further attacks on Jews.

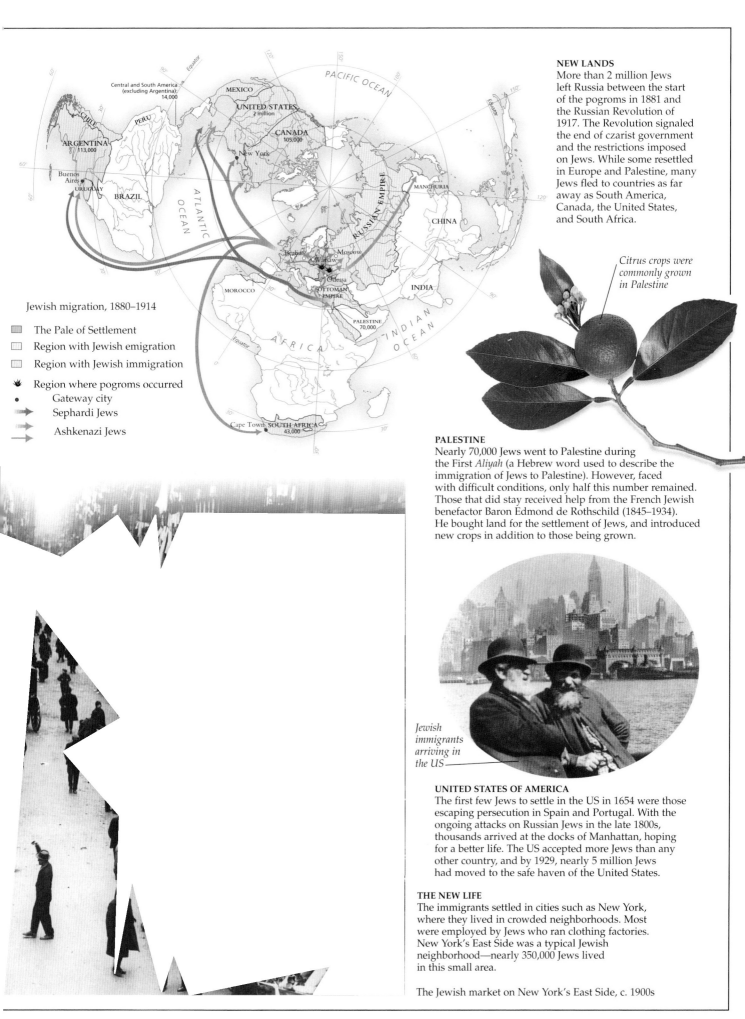

Jewish migration, 1880–1914

- ▢ The Pale of Settlement
- ▢ Region with Jewish emigration
- ▢ Region with Jewish immigration
- ✾ Region where pogroms occurred
- • Gateway city
- → Sephardi Jews
- → Ashkenazi Jews

Central and South America (excluding Argentina): 14,000

MEXICO

UNITED STATES 2 million

CANADA 105,000

New York

ARGENTINA 113,000

Buenos Aires

URUGUAY

BRAZIL

PERU

CHILE

ATLANTIC OCEAN

PACIFIC OCEAN

RUSSIAN EMPIRE

Berlin · Moscow
Warsaw
Odessa
OTTOMAN EMPIRE

MANCHURIA

CHINA

INDIA

MOROCCO

PALESTINE 70,000

AFRICA

INDIAN OCEAN

Cape Town SOUTH AFRICA 43,000

NEW LANDS

More than 2 million Jews left Russia between the start of the pogroms in 1881 and the Russian Revolution of 1917. The Revolution signaled the end of czarist government and the restrictions imposed on Jews. While some resettled in Europe and Palestine, many Jews fled to countries as far away as South America, Canada, the United States, and South Africa.

Citrus crops were commonly grown in Palestine

PALESTINE

Nearly 70,000 Jews went to Palestine during the First *Aliyah* (a Hebrew word used to describe the immigration of Jews to Palestine). However, faced with difficult conditions, only half this number remained. Those that did stay received help from the French Jewish benefactor Baron Edmond de Rothschild (1845–1934). He bought land for the settlement of Jews, and introduced new crops in addition to those being grown.

Jewish immigrants arriving in the US

UNITED STATES OF AMERICA

The first few Jews to settle in the US in 1654 were those escaping persecution in Spain and Portugal. With the ongoing attacks on Russian Jews in the late 1800s, thousands arrived at the docks of Manhattan, hoping for a better life. The US accepted more Jews than any other country, and by 1929, nearly 5 million Jews had moved to the safe haven of the United States.

THE NEW LIFE

The immigrants settled in cities such as New York, where they lived in crowded neighborhoods. Most were employed by Jews who ran clothing factories. New York's East Side was a typical Jewish neighborhood—nearly 350,000 Jews lived in this small area.

The Jewish market on New York's East Side, c. 1900s

Zionism

THE WORD ZION, a biblical word, is often used as an alternative name for the Land of Israel. Zionism is the political movement that gained momentum in the 19th century as a result of the pogroms and the resurfacing of anti-Semitic views witnessed during the trial of a French Jew, Alfred Dreyfus. The Zionists believed that the only way to avoid persecution was to have their own homeland—the Land of Israel. This cause was taken up by Theodor Herzl, a journalist covering the Dreyfus trial. Herzl was instrumental in setting up the First Zionist Congress in 1897. Later, the Jewish National Fund was established to buy land in Palestine. The Zionists were further helped when Britain took control of Palestine during World War I (1914–18), and made a promise to back Jewish settlement in Palestine.

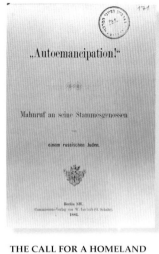

THE CALL FOR A HOMELAND
In 1882 Leon Pinkser (1821–91) wrote his pamphlet *Autoemancipation* (above). He described anti-Semitism as a disease and said the only cure for it was to allow Jews to create a homeland. The idea of Zionism dates back nearly 2,500 years, when the exiled Jews of Babylon yearned to return to their homeland. In the 1800s, Zionism became an important political force.

Alfred Dreyfus had his stripes removed and his sword broken as part of a military humiliation

THE DREYFUS AFFAIR
Alfred Dreyfus (1859–1935), a captain in the French army, was wrongly accused of treason in 1894. He was found guilty and imprisoned for life. A victim of anti-Semitism, Dreyfus was supported by important members of French society, such as the writer Emile Zola (1840–1902). However, it was not until 1906 that Dreyfus was finally cleared of all blame.

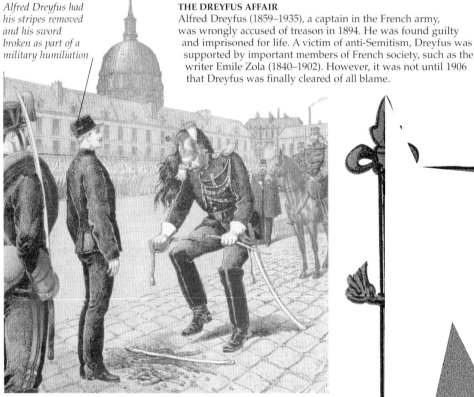

Theodor Herzl, who helped to found the Zionist movement

THE SOLUTION
Theodor Herzl (1860–1904), a Hungarian-born Jew, was shocked by the anti-Semitic treatment of Alfred Dreyfus. Herzl realized the need for a solution to the anti-Semitism still faced by Jews, even in countries where they had been granted equal rights. In 1896, he published his book, *The Jewish State*. Herzl called for the establishment of a Jewish state in Palestine—this was the only solution.

Herzl's suggestion for a Jewish flag was adopted by the Zionist Congress

THE FIRST ZIONIST CONGRESS
Not all Jews, especially those living in Western Europe, agreed with Herzl's solution. Many felt that his views would lead to further anti-Semitism. Nonetheless, the First Zionist Congress took place in 1897. The Congress called for the resettlement of Jews in Palestine, and set up the World Zionist Organization to put its goals into practice.

גאולה תתנו לארץ
ע"י קרן קימת לישראל

RESETTLEMENT

The Jewish National Fund, established in 1901 to buy land for Jews, helped the immigrants who made up the Second *Aliyah* (1904–14). Many resettled in the cities, while others tried to farm the land. One group of immigrants set up a farming community, where all the work and produce was shared equally. This laid the foundations of the *kibbutz*—unique to Israel then as it is now.

Tel Aviv in the 1920s

DEVELOPMENT OF THE CITIES

In 1909 the town of Tel Aviv was founded to house the increasing number of immigrants. It was the first all-Jewish city. The settlers were provided with funds for the building work, which they carried out themselves. By 1914, the flourishing city had over 1,000 people. In the same year, the number of Jewish inhabitants in Jerusalem totaled 45,000. The Zionists planned to build the first Hebrew University in Jerusalem, a goal finally realized in 1925.

Poster issued by the Jewish National Fund, calling for a return to the Land of Israel

THE BALFOUR DECLARATION

During World War I, Great Britain hoped to win Jewish support for its war efforts. In 1917 the Balfour Declaration was drafted by Lord Arthur Balfour (1848–1930), the British foreign secretary. The Declaration recognized the right of Jews to live in Palestine. This was a major landmark for the Zionists. In 1918, Britain conquered Palestine, which had been part of the Turkish Ottoman Empire since 1516. With a mandate to rule Palestine, the British were now responsible for implementing the Declaration.

Lord Balfour is shown on this commemorative version of the Balfour Declaration

A new nightmare

NAZI POSTER
The poster above was one of many issued by the Nazis. It reads, "One Europe's freedom," promoting the idea that Nazi rule was the only answer for Europe.

IN 1933 ADOLF HITLER (1889–1945) became chancellor of Germany. This was the start of a slowly unfolding tragedy for Jews throughout the world. Hitler's right-wing Nazi Party was driven by its program of hate—the elimination of Jews. Step by step, the Nazis put this policy into practice. A campaign of lies (propaganda) was launched against Jews. Schoolchildren were taught Nazi policies, while their parents were told to boycott Jewish shops. Anti-Jewish laws were passed, and many Jews were attacked or murdered. By 1937 over a hundred thousand Jews had fled from Germany, while Hitler marched into neighboring countries, signaling the same fate for their Jews.

ECONOMIC STEPS
In April 1933, a one-day boycott of Jewish shops was organized by the Nazis. The people were led to believe that Jews were greedy capitalists, and the best way to strike back was not to buy from them. Nazi guards stood outside some Jewish shops, and signs were also placed outside warning people not to enter. The sign above reads, "Germany! Resist! Do not buy from Jews!"

SPREADING LIES
Propaganda played a crucial part in the success of the Nazi regime. All forms of media, such as leaflets, radio, films, and posters, were used to show Jews as an inferior race and the cause of Germany's economic problems. A minister of propaganda was also appointed to promote the lies. By changing the minds of the people, the Nazis believed that they could then put their policies into action with very little resistance.

Detail from a Nazi leaflet designed to imply that Jews had built walls to divide people

BURNING BOOKS
In 1933 and 1936, the Nazis raided libraries and bookshops. Thousands of books were taken away. Many were written by Jews, but there were also books by non-Jewish writers, such as US author Ernest Hemingway, who did not agree with Nazi policies. The German people were encouraged to show their anti-Semitic feelings by burning the books.

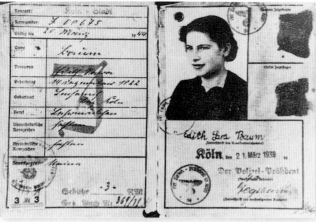

Passport of a Jewish woman

ANTI–SEMITISM IN SCHOOLS

The Nazis realized that it was important to win the minds of young children for the future survival of the Nazi Party. In schools, books were rewritten to further the cause of anti-Semitism. German children were taught that they belonged to the Aryan race (the superior fair-skinned, fair-haired race). By 1939, all children under the age of 18 years had to join the Nazi Youth Organization. Eventually, both Jewish teachers and children were forced out of German schools.

This detail from a Nazi schoolbook shows German children as the superior race

THE "J" STAMP

By the end of 1933, nearly 38,000 Jews had left Germany, mainly bound for England or the US. Between 1934 and 1939 a further 210,000 left, all having to pay large sums of money for their freedom. Their travel documents were stamped with the letter "J." The Hebrew name of Israel was added to every Jewish man and Sarah to every Jewish woman in an attempt to humiliate them. But these people were the lucky ones. After 1939, Jews were not able to leave Germany.

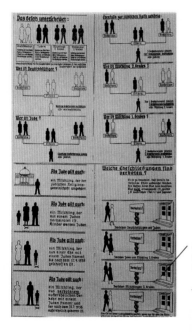

KRISTALLNACHT

In 1938, the Nazis launched their first full-scale attack on Jewish communities. Synagogues were set on fire, and Jewish homes were vandalized, as were Jewish shops and factories. This destruction was known as *Kristallnacht* (meaning "night of the broken glass"). Thousands of Jews were arrested and many were murdered. Soon, neighboring countries were invaded by the Nazi army. Jews in these countries were subjected to the same brutality and persecution faced by German Jews. The 1939 invasion of Poland, home to nearly 3 million Jews, sealed the desperate fate of European Jews.

Detailed charts were issued to show how to implement the Nuremberg Laws

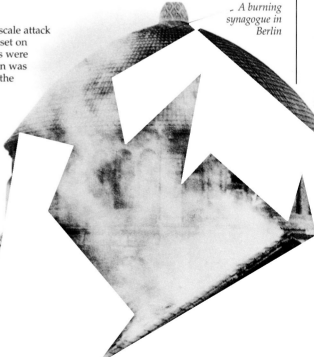

A burning synagogue in Berlin

THE NUREMBERG LAWS

During Nazi rule, laws were introduced to restrict the freedom of Jews. The worst of the anti-Jewish laws were known as the Nuremberg Laws of 1935. Jews were barred from marrying non-Jews and from taking up professional jobs such as teaching. The aim was to isolate Jews from all walks of German life, socially and economically. These laws were also introduced in countries occupied by the Nazis.

The charred remains of a synagogue—one of 600 to be reduced to ashes

The Holocaust

THE YELLOW STAR
From 1942 onward all Jews in Nazi-occupied Europe had to wear the yellow Star of David. This was designed to degrade all Jews (an act that can be traced back to the Middle Ages). The yellow color symbolized shame. Every Jew over the age of ten years had to wear the badge or face being shot.

THE TERM HOLOCAUST is used to describe the worst genocide that took place during World War II (1939–45). This mass extermination was the attempt by the Nazis to eradicate all Jews. Six million Jews were murdered, along with other people considered to be undesirable. The steps taken to wipe out the Jewish population of Europe varied from one Nazi-occupied country to another, but were more brutal in Eastern Europe. For Jews living in countries under direct Nazi rule, their prospect for survival was bleak. They were rounded up and confined to ghettos until they could be transported to the labor or death camps. Despite the hopelessness of their situation, Jewish resistance groups emerged. There were also many non-Jewish people who risked their lives to protect Jewish people.

Auschwitz concentration camp

THE WARSAW GHETTO UPRISING
The best-known example of Jewish resistance was the Warsaw ghetto uprising (nearly 445,000 Jews were crammed into this filthy ghetto in Poland). The rebellion started in 1943 when a group of Jewish fighters obtained arms and attacked German soldiers. But it was not long before the Germans forced the people out of their bunkers by burning the buildings. It has been estimated that 7,000 Jews in the ghetto were killed. Those who survived were sent to the death camps.

CONCENTRATION CAMPS
At first, the Nazis set up mobile death units to carry out their extermination plans. These death squads moved from area to area, killing Jews. Later, concentration camps were built for mass killings. The main death camps were in Poland, notably Auschwitz and Treblinka. Auschwitz was by far the largest of the death camps, where up to 12,000 Jews a day were killed.

This tin from Auschwitz contained cyanide gas crystals

THE GAS CHAMBER
It was from Auschwitz that the Nazis perfected their extermination method. In 1941, gas crystals were used to kill some of the victims in a makeshift gas chamber. But by the end of 1942, the Nazis converted two farmhouses into gas chambers, which worked day and night. These gas chambers could kill several hundred people at a time. Then, in 1943, the Nazis built four gas chambers that could kill 2,000 people at once.

Survivors are rounded up by the Nazis

PRISONERS AT AUSCHWITZ
Upon arrival, men, women, and children were forced to wear ill-fitting, filthy uniforms. Conditions at the camp were so inhumane that many prisoners died as a result.

Anne Frank

THE STORY OF ANNE FRANK
Anne Frank was a young girl when her parents decided to leave Germany to escape Hitler's anti-Jewish policies. They moved to Amsterdam, in the Netherlands. In 1942, when Anne was 13, the family hid in an annex above her father's business premises. She was given a small book that she used as a diary. Most of the Frank family, including Anne, perished in Auschwitz when they were discovered by the Nazis. After the war her diary was found and published in 1947. Since then the diary has been translated into more than 50 languages.

The diary kept by Anne Frank

> "If I just think of how we live here, I usually come to the conclusion that it is a paradise compared with how other Jews who are not in hiding must be living."
>
> **ANNE FRANK**

THE UNIFORM
The prisoners of Auschwitz had numbers tattooed on their left forearms for identification. Names were not used because the aim was to dehumanize the victims. Prisoners wore uniforms that had a triangular badge sewn on the front: yellow for Jews, red for political prisoners, green for criminals, brown for gypsies, and pink for homosexuals.

The remains of Schindler's factory, Poland

Oskar Schindler

ACTS OF HEROISM
Thousands of individuals risked their lives to help save the lives of Jews. Those who were well-connected, such as the Swedish diplomat Raul Wallenberg (1913–45), used their position to issue false documents and passports. But many of the individuals who helped came from ordinary walks of life. In France, Father Pierre-Marie Benoit (1895–1990), a monk from Marseilles, helped to smuggle thousands of Jewish children out of France and into Switzerland or Spain. Oskar Schindler (1908–74), a factory owner, employed Jewish prisoners. By doing so, he saved over a thousand people from certain death.

The aftermath

WORLD WAR II ended in May 1945 and so did the Holocaust. The aftermath revealed that one-third of the world's Jewish population had been killed as part of Hitler's plan. The war also displaced millions of Jewish people throughout Europe, and fearing repercussions, many did not want to return to their homes. Displaced Persons' (DP) camps were set up to provide shelter for them, while the perpetrators of the Holocaust were put on trial. Once again, the call for a Jewish homeland gathered momentum, resulting in the creation of the State of Israel in 1948. Sadly, this did not bring the peace and security that was hoped for.

THE SURVIVORS
It has been estimated that about 200,000 Jewish people survived the Holocaust by either hiding or pretending to be non-Jews. Children were often left with Christian families to be looked after, while others were taken to convents. The picture above is of Henri Obstfeld, who survived because he was hidden from the Nazis. Henri's parents did not see him for nearly three years.

This story book was sent to Henri by his parents when he was hiding

DISPLACED PERSONS
The war left over 1.5 million people without homes. Known as Displaced Persons, nearly 250,000 of these were Jews. Some returned to their homes to rebuild their lives. But this was not to prove easy— anti-Semitism did not end with the war. For example, Jews returning to Poland found their homes occupied, and many were attacked. The majority of the survivors found refuge in Displaced Persons' camps, where they were provided with much-needed food and medicine.

ער האט שוין פארגעסן, און גייט אין א ניעם גלות!
געדיינק ייד, יעדער גלות פירט צום אונטערגאנג.

שוין גענוג! בויל א היים!

Mother with her children at a Displaced Persons' camp

Zionist poster calling for survivors to go to Palestine instead of other countries

NEW HOMES
Five years after the Holocaust, there were still survivors with nowhere to go. The Zionists hoped to resettle as many of the Displaced Persons in Palestine as was possible. But Great Britain, which still had a mandate to govern Palestine, would only admit 13,000 of them. As a result, many of the Holocaust survivors were smuggled into Palestine, often through dangerous routes. Nearly 70,000 Jews entered Palestine in this way.

NUREMBERG TRIALS

In 1945, the Allied Forces (Great Britain, the US, France, and the Soviet Union) agreed to bring 22 high-ranking Nazis to trial in Germany. In what became known as the Nuremberg Trials, the Nazis were charged with committing crimes against humanity. The trials lasted 11 months, and judgments included death sentences, imprisonment, and acquittals. To this day, trials against the perpetrators continue. Many may never be found, since they changed their names and fled to other countries to avoid being caught.

THE STATE OF ISRAEL

The pressure to find a homeland for the survivors was considerable. Many wanted to return to Palestine, but were unable to do so. In 1948, Great Britain withdrew its forces from Palestine, thus ending its mandate. Despite fierce opposition from Arab governments, the United Nations decided that Palestine was to be divided to create the State of Israel. Almost 50 years later, Theodor Herzl's dream had been realized.

Children wave the new flags of the State of Israel, in England in 1948

NEW CONFLICTS

Thousands of Jews made the journey to the new State of Israel. The people included survivors of the war and Jews from countries outside Europe who wanted to return to their ancient homeland. Between 1948 to 1951, nearly 700,000 immigrants settled in the new state. However, since 1948, Israel has survived many wars, including the War of Independence (1948), the Six-Day War (1967), and the *Yom Kippur* War (1973). In the war of 1967, East Jerusalem was captured by the Israeli army, giving Jews access to one of the holiest places, the Western Wall. The important victory is celebrated on Jerusalem Day.

Israelis celebrate the first Jerusalem Day, 1968

THE PAST

Memorials have been built in many countries as a reminder of the millions of lives lost during the Holocaust. For many people, it is important to remember the horrors of the past. In Israel, people remember the tragedy on *Yom Hashoah* (Holocaust Day).

Holocaust memorial of a hand reaching to the sky, South Beach, Florida

The synagogue

THE SYNAGOGUE IS AN IMPORTANT place of worship and center of Jewish life. Derived from the Greek word meaning "place of assembly," the synogogue was essential to the survival of the Jewish faith. When the Second Temple was destroyed in 70 CE, the rabbis developed the idea of a house of worship in order to keep the faith alive among the people of the Diaspora. The importance of the Temple has never been forgotten. Even today, when a synagogue is built, a section of a wall is sometimes left unplastered to serve as a reminder of the Temple's destruction. Unlike the Christian church, there is no set style for the exterior design of the synagogue. Often the architecture reflects the culture of the country in which it is built. The layout inside, however, follows a common pattern.

Each minaret stands 141 feet (43 meters) tall

A PLACE FOR STUDY AND PRAYER
Another name for a synagogue is *Bet Hamidrash*, meaning "House of Study." This is a reminder of the close relationship between prayer and *Torah* study. Synagogues hold classes where older boys and young men can study rabbinic texts.

AN ORNATE SYNAGOGUE
The Dohany Synagogue in Budapest, Hungary, is the largest synagogue in Europe, accommodating up to 3,000 people. Built in 1859, the synagogue reflects Islamic influences with its decorative features and minaret-like towers.

Model of the Kaifeng Synagogue

THE PAGODA SYNAGOGUE
One of the most unusual houses of worship was the Kaifeng Synagogue of China. It was first built in 1163 by the descendants of Jewish silk merchants from Persia (modern Iran). The synagogue was rebuilt several times, but by the mid-1800s, the Jewish community in China had declined, and the synagogue was demolished.

Hechal Yehuda Synagogue

A MODERN SYNAGOGUE
This Sephardi synagogue in Tel Aviv, Israel, was designed with the hot climate in mind. Built from concrete, the white, shell-like exterior reflects the heat, while cool air circulates around the cavernous interior. In Israel, there is a mixture of ancient and modern synagogues existing side by side.

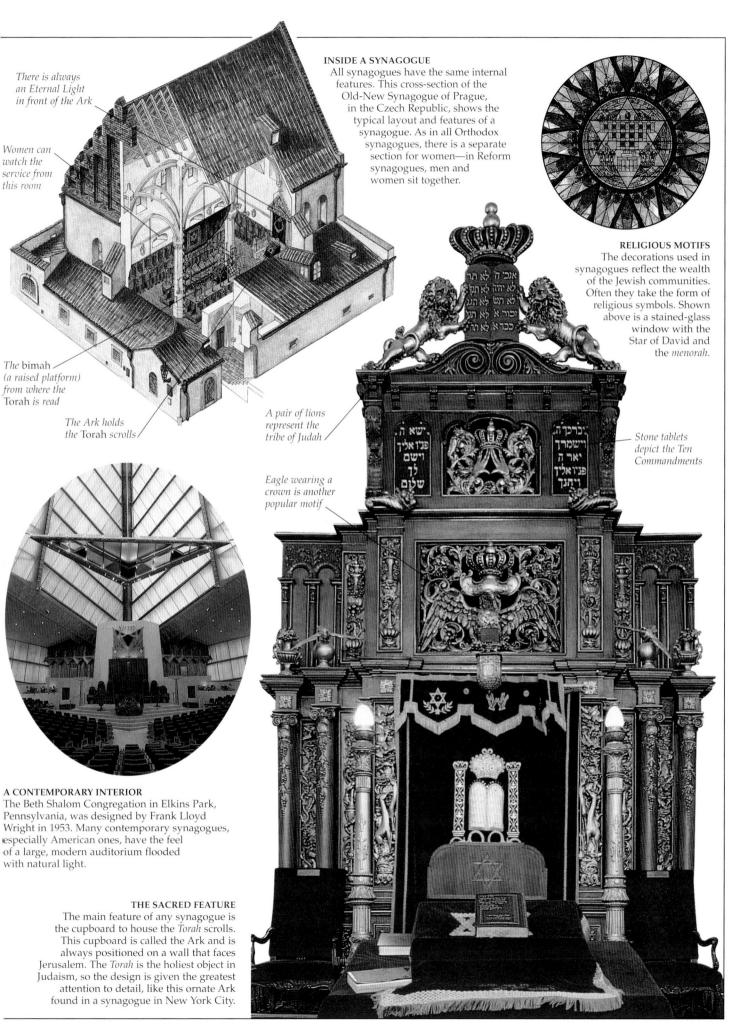

There is always an Eternal Light in front of the Ark

Women can watch the service from this room

The bimah *(a raised platform) from where the* Torah *is read*

The Ark holds the Torah *scrolls*

A pair of lions represent the tribe of Judah

Eagle wearing a crown is another popular motif

INSIDE A SYNAGOGUE
All synagogues have the same internal features. This cross-section of the Old-New Synagogue of Prague, in the Czech Republic, shows the typical layout and features of a synagogue. As in all Orthodox synagogues, there is a separate section for women—in Reform synagogues, men and women sit together.

RELIGIOUS MOTIFS
The decorations used in synagogues reflect the wealth of the Jewish communities. Often they take the form of religious symbols. Shown above is a stained-glass window with the Star of David and the *menorah*.

Stone tablets depict the Ten Commandments

A CONTEMPORARY INTERIOR
The Beth Shalom Congregation in Elkins Park, Pennsylvania, was designed by Frank Lloyd Wright in 1953. Many contemporary synagogues, especially American ones, have the feel of a large, modern auditorium flooded with natural light.

THE SACRED FEATURE
The main feature of any synagogue is the cupboard to house the *Torah* scrolls. This cupboard is called the Ark and is always positioned on a wall that faces Jerusalem. The *Torah* is the holiest object in Judaism, so the design is given the greatest attention to detail, like this ornate Ark found in a synagogue in New York City.

Prayer

Prayer is central to Judaism, as it is in other religions. Jews are supposed to pray three times a day—morning, afternoon, and night. Prayers can be recited alone, but it is preferable to pray with a group of at least ten people (or ten men in an Orthodox community), called a *minyan*. The prayers are contained in a book called a *siddur,* and the most famous prayer is the *Shema*, which declares the supremacy of God. Although there is no Jewish law dictating the dress code, male Jews normally wear a head covering, known as a *kippa* or *yarmulka*, and a *tallit* (prayer shawl) to pray. For morning services, other than those on *Shabbat* or a festival, a *tefillin* (two small boxes containing sacred text) is also worn. Women may wear some or all of these items in non-Orthodox communities.

MEZUZAH
The *mezuzah* is a small container holding a piece of parchment on which the words of the *Shema* are written. It can be made of any material and is often highly decorated. The *mezuzah* is placed on the front door of a Jewish house and sometimes on all the internal doors of the house, except the bathroom.

"Hear, O Israel, the Lord is our God, the Lord is one."

FIRST LINE OF THE SHEMA

TALLIT
A *tallit* may be beautifully embroidered and decorated, but the most important part are the tassels *(tzitzit)* on each of the four corners. The Book of Exodus mentions the wearing of these tassels as a visible sign of obedience to God. Jewish men, and in some cases women, wear a *tallit* to pray.

KIPPA
Some Jewish men only wear a *kippa* to pray, while others wear one all the time. It is considered respectful to cover one's head because it reminds the wearer that God is constantly present.

WESTERN WALL
The only remaining part of the Second Temple in Jerusalem, Israel, is known as the Western Wall. It is Judaism's holiest site and dates back to the 1st century CE. People come to pray at the wall, and frequently leave written messages in the spaces between the stones. The Western Wall used to be known as the Wailing Wall because it was the scene of so much weeping.

Sealed within each box are passages from the Torah *and the text of the* Shema

Tefillin *strapped around the forehead*

A right-handed person wears the tefillin *on the left arm*

TEFILLIN
During morning services, Orthodox men wear the *tefillin*. One box is attached to the forehead, and this is said to make the wearer think of his faith. The other box is strapped around the left arm, because this is closest to the heart.

The siddur

The leather straps are from a kosher *animal*

PRAYERS
In Judaism, there are prayers for all occasions. Many prayers are formal (based on verses in the *Torah)* and have to be said on special occasions, such as on the holy day of *Yom Kippur*. One of the most important prayers is called the *Shema*. This is generally the first prayer a Jewish child learns, and says every night before going to sleep. But it is also important for Jewish people to recite their own daily prayers, bringing them closer to God.

Each tassel has five knots to serve as a reminder of the Five Books of Moses

SIDDUR
In addition to all the prayers, the *siddur* contains many blessings to be said as part of daily life. The word *siddur* means "order," because the prayers are written in the order they are said for the services during the course of the year. It also reflects the fact that God created the world in a certain order.

Sacred books

THE HEBREW BIBLE consists of three books: the *Torah* (Hebrew word meaning "teaching"), *Nevi'im* (the Prophets), and *Ketuvim* (the Writings). The *Torah*, also known as the Five Books of Moses, is the most important in everyday Jewish life. Jews believe that the words of the *Torah* are the words of God as revealed to Moses on Mount Sinai 3,000 years ago. As well as the early history of Jewish religion, it gives instructions on every aspect of daily life, and religious Jews show their obedience to God by following these laws. The *Torah* is always treated with reverence, from the moment a scroll is written by a skilled scribe to its use in synagogue services.

THE FIVE BOOKS OF MOSES
Genesis is the first of the five books found in the *Torah*. It tells the story of how the world was created and covers the stories of Adam and Eve (shown above) and the patriarchs—Abraham, Isaac, and Jacob. Exodus, Leviticus, Numbers, and Deuteronomy form the rest of the *Torah*.

Sample parchment with Hebrew letters and signs

THE SCRIBE
The *Torah* has always been written by hand, even to this day. It can take a scribe, or *sofer*, over a year to copy accurately every word. A scribe has to be a religious Jew and must train for seven years. When the *Torah* scroll is completed, it has to be checked several times before it can be used in the synagogue.

Kosher quill

TOOLS OF THE TRADE
Certain tools are used when writing a *Torah* scroll. The ink has to be specially prepared, and only a quill from a *kosher* bird can be used to write the text. The parchment for the scroll also has to come from a *kosher* animal, which cannot be killed just for its hide.

Special ink

The text is written in columns

THE DEAD SEA SCROLLS

In 1947, fragments of ancient manuscripts were discovered in the caves of Qumran, near the Dead Sea, Israel. They consisted of text from almost every book of the Hebrew Bible. Written between 150 BCE and CE 68, the manuscripts would have belonged to the Essene community—an ancient Jewish sect. The discovery of the Dead Sea Scrolls shows that the Hebrew Bible has changed very little since Roman times.

This inkpot was found in Qumran and may have been used by the scribes

THE YAD

The *yad*, meaning "hand" in Hebrew, is used by the person reading from the *Torah* to point to the words. This is to preserve the handwritten text and prevent it from being damaged. If a single letter of the *Torah* is smudged, the scroll is no longer considered fit to be used unless it is repaired by a scribe.

THE TORAH

The *Torah* is the holiest book in Jewish life. It contains 613 commandments. These are instructions for Jews on how to live a good and pious life. From the time of Moses, the laws were passed by word of mouth. Later they were written down so they would not be forgotten. Orthodox Jews adhere strictly to all the laws of the *Torah*. But there are also many Jews who only follow those laws that they feel apply to modern life.

The Torah scroll is raised after the service and shown to the congregation

Handles are always used to unroll or hold the scroll

READING THE TORAH

The *Torah* scroll is read over the course of a year with a section chanted each *Shabbat* in the synagogue. Everyone in the congregation stands up as a mark of respect when the *Torah* is taken out of the Ark.

Writings and thinkers

THE IMPORTANCE OF learning has always been valued in Judaism, and the compilation of the *Talmud* and the *Midrash* illustrate this point. After the *Torah*, the *Talmud* has become the most important religious book. It was created over the years as thousands of rabbis studied the *Torah* and recorded their interpretations. Notable scholars also added comments to the wealth of religious thought and practices. One such figure was Maimonides, who was known for his theological and philosophical works. Scholars of a more mystical nature recorded the oral traditions that became the *Kabbalah*. Another book, the *Haggadah*, recounts the story of the Exodus from Egypt and has become an integral part of Jewish life.

Noah's ark

THE MIDRASH
The *Midrash* is a collection of writings that helps to explain the stories of the Hebrew Bible, such as Noah's ark and Jonah. Written by rabbis, their goal is to teach moral lessons.

THE TALMUD
The *Talmud* is a compilation of Jewish laws with explanations provided by Jewish scholars. Completed in the 5th century, the writings cover every aspect of Jewish life, from prayers to business disputes. Subsequent rabbis added their own commentaries. One of the most famous was French-born Rabbi Rashi (1040–1105).

The main text is always in the center of the page

Commentaries from various rabbis appear around the page

"What is hateful to you do not do to your neighbor. That is the whole Torah—the rest is commentary."

TRACTATE SHABBAT 31A, THE TALMUD

MAIMONIDES
Rabbi Moses ben Maimon (1138–1204), known as Maimonides, was a distinguished philosopher and physician. Born in Spain, Maimonides settled in Egypt, where he wrote the *Mishnah Torah*, a review of all Jewish religious laws based on the *Talmud*. He also attempted to reconcile Jewish faith with reason, based on the teachings of Greek philosopher Aristotle.

> *"Before God manifested Himself, when all things were still hidden in Him He began by forming an imperceptible point—that was His own thought. With this thought He then began to construct a mysterious and holy form—the Universe."*
>
> **THE ZOHAR**

THE HAGGADAH
Dating from the time of King Solomon's reign (c. 10th century BCE) the *Haggadah*, meaning "narrative," recounts the story of the Exodus from Egypt. It also contains blessings and psalms, and is always read before the Passover meal. The illustration above is from a children's *Haggadah*, showing the ten plagues sent by God to punish the Egyptians.

This is one of the earliest examples of an Ashkenazi Haggadah

THE BOOK OF SPLENDOR
In Judaism, the term *Kabbalah* (meaning "tradition") represents an alternative mystical view of the world based on the *Torah*. The ideas were passed on by word of mouth and kept secret. The *Zohar*, or *Book of Splendor*, is the most important text for followers of the *Kabbalah*, introducing new rituals. The book is attributed to Moses de Leon, a *Kabbalist* who lived in Spain during the 13th century.

SEFIROT
In the *Zohar*, the *Kabbalah* is explained in terms of 10 creative forces, known as the *sefirot*. These are the 10 attributes by which God has created the Universe. The *sefirot* are shown as branches of a tree, and include love, wisdom, power, intelligence, and beauty.

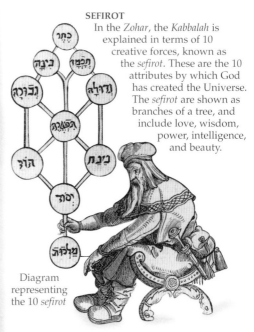

Diagram representing the 10 sefirot

BIRD'S HEAD HAGGADAH
This famous *Haggadah* from 13th-century Germany is illustrated with biblical scenes. As the name suggests, most of the human figures are drawn with birds' heads. Today, a *Haggadah* may illustrate contemporary events such as the creation of the State of Israel, or convey the socialist ideas of the *kibbutz*.

Values

For observant Jews, the *Torah* is more than just learning about the early history of Judaism and following a set of religious beliefs. It provides a moral blueprint on how to live good and honest lives. Not only are there laws governing a person's relationship with God, but there are also laws about how to treat other people. Several fundamental values are addressed in the *Torah*—the sanctity of life, justice and equality, kindness and generosity, the value of education, and social responsibility. One of the most frequent commands in the *Torah* is the *mitzvah* (commandment) of showing kindness to strangers. Jews have lived without a homeland for thousands of years, and they know what it is like to be a stranger in a foreign land. However, it is the value of human life that takes precedence, to the extent that many of the commandments may be broken to protect life. Such values are as relevant today as they were in biblical times, and are seen as an essential part of any democracy.

Prophet Jeremiah

JUSTICE AND EQUALITY
Over 2,000 years ago, Jewish people were already governed by a system of checks and balances. Power to govern was not vested in the hands of the king. It was left to the *Sanhedrin* (the Jewish Supreme Court) to interpret the laws of the *Torah* and apply them fairly. The prophets also rebuked those who were seen to act against the interests of the people.

RESPECT FOR LIFE
Judaism emphasizes the value of human life. The life of one person is no less important than the life of another. This concern for life also extends to animals. One of the oldest laws prohibiting cruelty to animals is found in the *Torah*. In many Jewish homes, the creation of the world is remembered during *Shabbat*.

HOSPITALITY
The obligation to look after travelers and strangers is central to Judaism. Abraham, regarded as the first Jew, and his wife Sarah were always hospitable and set the tone for future generations. During the Middle Ages many Jewish villages had a guest house where traveling beggars could stay for free. One rabbi in the *Talmud* even voiced the opinion that welcoming guests is more important than welcoming God by studying the *Torah*.

Stained-glass detail of Abraham

REPAIRING THE WORLD
Loving your neighbor as yourself is a biblical instruction. Man was created in the image of God, and so individuals must be treated with the utmost respect and honor. Ignorance and intolerance darken the world, but understanding and love bring light and help to restore the world.

Hanukkah menorah *symbolizes the triumph of good over evil*

Charity boxes are often seen in Jewish homes

CHARITY
The Hebrew term *tzedakah* is used to describe charitable acts, and it is seen as the duty of every person to share what God has given them. Every week, before the start of *Shabbat*, coins are dropped into a charity box, and on festivals such as *Purim*, collections are taken for various charities. According to Maimonides, the best act of *tzedakah* is helping someone to help themselves by teaching them a skill.

EDUCATION
The importance of knowledge is stressed by the *Torah*. Education is not only seen as a means of achieving a worthwhile career, but also as a way of teaching children how to behave correctly. The *Torah* says it is the duty of every individual to pursue a good quality of life, while being respectful to others and not following the path of greed.

Torah scroll and *yad*

SOCIAL RESPONSIBILITY
One of the commandments of Judaism is to look after the welfare of others, just as God had done by visiting Abraham when he was sick. The illustration above shows the biblical figure of Job, who endured much suffering, being visited by friends. The obligation to care for one another has prevailed in Jewish communities.

Kosher food

THERE ARE LAWS GOVERNING every aspect of Jewish life, and this extends to food. The dietary laws are known as *kashrut*, and they outline the foods that can be eaten and how they should be prepared. The word *kosher* (meaning "fit" or "proper") is used to describe food that complies with these laws. Religious objects, too, have to be made in accordance with the rules. Many of the dietary laws are mentioned in the *Torah*, and others come from rabbinic interpretations. As well as being a biblical command, the food laws also serve a hygienic function and form a strong source of group identity. The degree of observance varies among Jews, with some adhering to all the laws, while others only follow certain rules.

THE KOSHER SHOP
The laws of *kashrut* are complex, so it is far easier and safer for observant Jews to buy their food from *kosher* shops. The majority of the packaged foods have a *kosher* label to show that a rabbi has visited the factory and certified that the food has been prepared correctly.

MEAT AND DAIRY
Animals that have cloven hooves and chew the cud, such as lamb, are regarded as *kosher*, but pork is not. Animals have to be slaughtered by a trained person to minimize the amount of pain. Blood also needs to be drained from the meat, because it contains the life of the animal. Meat and dairy products cannot be eaten together, and a *kosher* household must have two sets of utensils and plates to keep meat and dairy products separate.

Lentils

PARVE FOOD
Foods that are neither dairy nor meat are known as *parve* and can be eaten with both kinds of meals. These foods include fruit, vegetables, rice, eggs, and lentils. But fruit and vegetables have to be checked thoroughly before consumption to make sure that there are no insects—the *Torah* considers all insects to be non-*kosher*.

*This **kosher** food stall only sells meat products, such stalls are found in areas where there is a large Jewish community*

Crab

Salmon

SEAFOOD
Only fish with both fins and scales, such as salmon, trout, and cod, are considered *kosher*. This means that all shellfish and other seafoods are not permitted. These forbidden foods are known as *treifah*.

Shofar

RELIGIOUS OBJECTS

The laws of *kashrut* are also applicable to ritual objects. These include the *shofar*, which has to be made from the horn of a *kosher* animal. The parchment found inside a *mezuzah* or used for the *Torah* scroll also has to come from a *kosher* animal.

PASSOVER

There are certain ingredients, that cannot be eaten during Passover. For identification purposes, some food packages have a *"Kosher* for Passover" label, such as the package above that contains unleavened bread.

THE VINEYARD

Considerable care must be taken when managing a *kosher* vineyard. The *Torah* instructs that grapes from a new vineyard cannot be used until the fourth year, and every seven years the vineyard has to be left fallow.

WINE PRODUCTION

In ancient times, Jews were forbidden to drink wine that may have been part of pagan worship, so they produced their own. Today, strict regulations apply to the production of *kosher* wine. For example, only observant Jews are allowed to oversee the production. The winery also has a supervising rabbi to make sure that all the requirements have been met before issuing a *kosher* certificate.

Torah scroll

Kosher wine

The faces of Judaism

THE MAJORITY OF JEWS TODAY are descendants of the Ashkenazi (Eastern European) or the Sephardi (Spanish). Within these two main cultural groups, there are several religious branches, which have developed over a period of time to meet the demands of contemporary life. The branches of Judaism differ in the strength of their beliefs, ranging from extreme Orthodox to those adopting a more liberal approach to life and religion. But because Judaism is more than just a faith, various customs and traditions have developed in the communities that exist around the world. For example, there is a considerable difference between the Jews of Ethiopia and those of Yemen. Essentially, what all Jews share is a common history and language, no matter what beliefs and customs they follow.

CONSERVATIVE
Solomon Schechter (1847–1915) (above) was the driving force behind the Conservative movement. Known as *Masorti* (meaning "tradition") in Israel, Conservative Jews take the middle ground between Orthodox and Reform Judaism.

Samaritan *Torah* scroll

REFORM
The movement known as Reform Judaism began in Germany during the 19th century. Reform Jews believe that the *Torah* and *Talmud* do not contain the literal words of God, but were written by people who were inspired by God. This means they can adapt their faith to suit modern life, such as improving the status of Jewish women. Reform Judaism is also known as Liberal or Progressive Judaism. This is the largest group of Jews in the US.

Female rabbi

An ultra-Orthodox Jew praying

ORTHODOX
Orthodox Jews follow their traditional practices and faith closely. The majority of Jews who live in Europe are Orthodox. But ultra-Orthodox Jews are one of the fastest-growing groups. Uncompromising in their religious beliefs, these Jews tend to live in separate communities with their own schools and courts of law. Generally, they feel it is wrong to mix with the outside world, even with less observant Jews. Within the ultra-Orthodox movement, there are various sects, each with their own leadership, such as the Lubavitch sect in the US.

Children in a *kibbutz* school, Israel

SAMARITANS
The Samaritan community in Israel can be traced back to the 7th century BCE. Although they do not consider themselves to be Jews, they practice a form of Judaism. Samaritans accept the authority of the Five Books of Moses, observe the *Shabbat*, and perform circumcision. Today, the Samaritan community living in Israel numbers up to 500 people.

JEWS IN ISRAEL
Israel is home to over 4 million Jews, the second-largest community outside the US. The Law of Return, which was passed by the Israeli government in 1950, allowed thousands of Jews to become citizens. Jews from countries throughout the world were all welcomed. At the same time, the immigrant communities in Israel have maintained the traditions of their country of origin. Today, a majority of Israelis consider themselves secular (nonreligious) Jews.

ETHIOPIAN JEWS
The origin of Jews from Ethiopia, known as *Beta Israel* ("House of Israel"), is a source of debate. Some Ethiopian Jews believe that they are the descendants of the son of King Solomon and the Queen of Sheba. Others believe that they belong to a lost tribe of Israel. Whatever their origins, the existence of Ethiopian Jews only came to light during the 1850s. To escape the famine in war-torn Ethiopia, almost the entire Jewish population was airlifted to Israel in the 1980s and 1990s.

Ethiopian Jews take part in a blessing for Passover

JEWS OF INDIA
The Jewish community of India is thought to have been founded over 2,000 years ago. There were three distinct groups: Bene Israel ("Jews of Israel"), the Cochin Jews, and those from European countries such as Spain. All groups followed Sephardi practices and had their own synagogues. Today, there are only a few thousand Indian Jews.

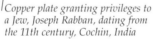
Copper plate granting privileges to a Jew, Joseph Rabban, dating from the 11th century, Cochin, India

Observant Yemenite Jews study the *Torah*

YEMENITE JEWS
There is evidence of Jews living in Yemen from the 1st century CE. Yemenite Jews have a very strong scholarly tradition and their own prayer book, called the *tiklal*. Most now live in Israel or the US, though a small number remain in Yemen.

Symbols and language

Jewish communities now exist in every part of the world, and the people have preserved their way of life and faith even while living beside non-Jews. Although Jews have their own language, they also adopted the language of the country in which they resided. But over a period of time, the spoken Hebrew language of the Israelites declined, though it survived through religious use. At the same time, two symbols of Judaism remain constant in representing the faith and identity of the Jewish people living in the Diaspora: the *menorah* and the *Magen David*.

HANUKKAH MENORAH
Only an eight-branched *menorah* can be used to celebrate the festival of *Hanukkah*—with an extra branch of the candlestick used to hold the servant candle, from which all other candles are lit. The eight-day festival commemorates the victory of Judah the Maccabee over the Seleucids.

SEVEN-BRANCHED MENORAH
The seven-branched *menorah* (Hebrew for "candlestick") is the oldest and most widely used symbol in Judaism. A golden *menorah* was kept in the Tabernacle and in the First and Second Temples. Since the destruction of the Temples, the *menorah* has remained an important expression of the faith.

The flag of Israel

The six points of the star represent the six days of creation

Blue represents heaven, and serves as a reminder of God's ways

White symbolizes purity and peace

STAR OF DAVID
In Hebrew, the Star of David is known as the *Magen David*. The six-pointed star was first used as a decorative feature during the Roman period, and in the 17th century the design was used to represent the Jewish community of Prague, in the Czech Republic. The star gained national significance when it was used in 1897 for the First Zionist Congress. Since the creation of the State of Israel in 1948, the six-pointed star is used on the national flag.

Stone carving of the Star of David, dating from the 4th century CE

Eliezer
Ben-Yehuda

SPOKEN HEBREW

During the late
19th century
there was a
revival in
spoken Hebrew.
Eliezer Ben-Yehuda
(1858–1922), a
Jewish settler in
the land of Israel,
decided to revive the
language, which evolved
into modern-day Hebrew. Tracing all
the words from the time of Abraham,
in 1910 Ben-Yehuda published the
first volume of his six-volume
Hebrew dictionary.

FORMS OF HEBREW

The nature of ancient Hebrew changed when Jews settled in new
countries. Spoken Hebrew was influenced by the language of the host
country, and this resulted in several versions of Hebrew. Jews who
settled in Spain and Portugal during the Middle Ages spoke a
form of Hebrew known as Ladino. In Eastern Europe, Yiddish
was widely spoken and remained so until the 20th century.

*The seven
branches
represent the
days of the week*

Ancient Hebrew scroll

The first ten letters
of the Hebrew
alphabet

THE ALPHABET

A 22-letter alphabet was already
being used when the Israelites
settled in Canaan. The alphabet
provided a simple way of recording
events. When the Israelites were
exiled in the 8th century BCE,
Hebrew was written in a square
script, which still prevails today.

LANGUAGE OF ISRAEL

Modern Hebrew is the
official language of the
State of Israel. Nearly
4 million Israelis speak
it as their first language.
Many Hebrew words,
such as *amen* and
hallelujah, have also
filtered into other
languages.

*This Coca-Cola
label is written in
modern Hebrew*

WRITTEN HEBREW

Hebrew is written from right to left.
Children learn to read and write with
the vowels, which are represented by little
marks that surround the main script. But
in printed Hebrew, the vowels are often
left out. Although most Jews speak the
language of the country they live in,
it is still important for them to be
able to read Hebrew prayers in
synagogue services.

Front cover of the *Jewish News*

PRINTED HEBREW

The 19th century saw the publication
of many Hebrew newspapers,
advertisements, and labels for
a variety of products. The written
form of Hebrew was no longer
being used just for religious books.

Through a Jewish lifetime

IN JUDAISM, KEY LIFE EVENTS are marked with special ceremonies. The circumcision of baby boys is a universal Jewish custom, dating back to biblical times. More recently, people have also begun to welcome baby girls with a baby-naming ceremony. *Bar* and *Bat Mitzvah* mark the point at which children become adult members of the community. Some Reform Jewish communities also celebrate a coming of age for both sexes at 15 or 16 in a ceremony called confirmation. There are specific Jewish customs marking marriage, and also surrounding death and mourning. All these life-cycle events are celebrated publicly, stressing the communal nature of Jewish life.

BAR AND BAT MITZVAH PRESENTS
This *siddur* is designed to be given to a girl on her *Bat Mitzvah*. Although gifts are often given to mark the occasion, a *Bar* or *Bat Mitzvah* is not about presents, but about taking on the responsibilities of a Jewish adult.

Birth

In addition to an English name, every Jewish child is given a Hebrew name, which will be used for the rites of passage. Often, the Hebrew name will be the same as that of a relative who has recently died. The Hebrew name of a baby boy is announced at his *Brit Milah* (circumcision) ceremony, while that of a baby girl is announced in the synagogue on the first *Shabbat* after her birth or, alternatively, at a special baby-naming ceremony.

Paper amulet, Morocco, 20th century

CIRCUMCISION AMULETS
In former times, circumcision amulets were used by some communities to protect newborn babies against evil. These small pieces of parchment, paper, or metal were inscribed with magical signs, combinations of letters, names of angels or of God. They were worn or placed on a wall near the baby's crib. Many rabbis, including Maimonides, opposed such amulets as mere superstition.

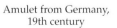

Amulet from Germany, 19th century

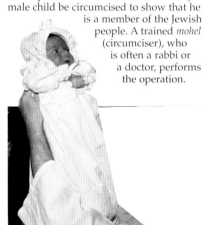

CIRCUMCISION CEREMONY
Brit milah is carried out on the eighth day after the birth of a boy. It dates back to God's promise with Abraham that every male child be circumcised to show that he is a member of the Jewish people. A trained *mohel* (circumciser), who is often a rabbi or a doctor, performs the operation.

48

Coming of Age

At the age of 13, a boy is considered to be *Bar Mitzvah* ("son of the commandment"), and becomes responsible for his religious actions. For example, he must fast on *Yom Kippur*, and he may be counted as part of the *minyan* in the synagogue. A girl is considered to be *Bat Mizvah* ("daughter of the commandment") at 12 years old. Depending on her community, she may or may not participate in a *minyan* or read from the *Torah*.

This woman wears a tallit *and a* kippa *for her ceremony*

BAT MITZVAH
Bat Mitzvah ceremonies for girls did not develop until the beginning of the 20th century. Today, this rite of passage can be marked in different ways, ranging from one in which the girl reads from the *Torah*, exactly the same as boys do, to an Orthodox *Bat Chayil*, where the girl gives a sermon in the synagogue. Some Orthodox communities do not publicly mark *Bat Mitzvah*.

Tefillin

TEFILLIN
An Orthodox boy will be given a set of *tefillin* for his *Bar Mitzvah*. From then on he is expected to pray every weekday morning wearing the *tefillin*. When not being worn, they are kept in a bag, which may be decorated with the owner's name in Hebrew.

Tefillin *case with the boy's name in Hebrew*

A boy reads from the Torah *during a weekday ceremony*

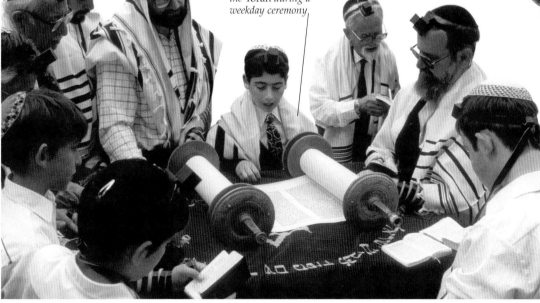

BAR MITZVAH
At a *Bar Mitzvah* ceremony, the boy is called to read a section from the *Torah*, which he has prepared in advance. This symbolizes his acceptance of the commandments. In very observant communities, a boy may read the entire *sidra* (portion) for that week—normally four to six chapters long. The *Bar Mitzvah* is celebrated after the synagogue service, where most boys also give a speech called a *dvar Torah* ("word of *Torah*").

Continued from previous page

The huppah *is depicted in this ancient* Torah *binder*

Marriage

Observant Jews see marriage as a gift from God, and it is an important religious occasion. The marriage is the start of a new home, and, often, a new family to ensure that the practices and traditions of Judaism continue. Ceremonies vary depending on whether the service is Orthodox or Reform, and there are also different local customs. Generally, Jewish weddings can take place anywhere—in a synagogue, at home, or in the open air.

BREAKING THE GLASS
The end of the ceremony is marked by the groom breaking a wine glass. This symbolizes the destruction of the Temple and the fragility of marriage. The picture above shows a Reform service, where both the bride and groom share the symbolic gesture.

THE HUPPAH
The main service is conducted by a rabbi under the *huppah*, a cloth canopy supported by four poles. In some Jewish communities, a prayer shawl is held over the bride and groom. The *huppah* symbolizes the couple's new home.

The ketubah *is beautifully decorated with motifs or biblical scenes*

THE KETUBAH
The Jewish marriage contract, which details the obligations of the groom toward his bride, is called a *ketubah*. It is signed by the groom at the start of the ceremony, although in modern weddings both the bride and groom sign the document. The *ketubah* is read during the marriage service, and decorative ones are often displayed at home.

The ornate headdress contains the herb rue to ward off evil

WEDDING CUSTOMS
In many Jewish weddings, it is customary for the bride to wear white and sometimes also the groom. In contrast, Yemenite Jews dress in highly ornate clothing, as illustrated.

WEDDING RING
The exchange of wedding rings was a Roman practice adopted by various faiths, including Judaism. In traditional Jewish weddings the groom places a ring on the bride's finger and blessings are recited. In the past, some Jewish communities would loan the bride a magnificent ring, often decorated with a miniature house and inscribed with the words *Mazel Tov* ("Good Luck").

Ornate Italian wedding ring

AN OLD CUSTOM
Traditionally, a father would begin saving almost from the time his daughter was born so he could give her a dowry. In the case of orphans or girls from very poor families, the Jewish community would pool together to provide basic items for a dowry. In modern families, this is not considered necessary.

This necklace belonged to a Jewish bride from Bokhara, Uzbekistan, and dates from the 19th century

BRIDAL CASKET
In the past, the bride would be given gifts by the groom. The *ketubah* contained a clause saying that if the couple divorced, the woman would be able to claim these possessions as her own. This made Judaism an enlightened religion, because for centuries, Christian or Muslim wives had no formal right to any property in the event of a divorce. This bridal casket was a gift to a Jewish bride by her wealthy groom.

15th-century bridal casket, Italy

Death customs

The traditional customs associated with the last rite of passage have two purposes: to show respect for the dead and to help the grieving process. Mourners usually express their initial grief by making a tear in their clothing. It is also important for the deceased to be buried promptly (usually within three days). However, some Jews today prefer cremation. The funeral services are simple affairs, so that there is no distinction between a rich and a poor person's ceremony.

MARK OF RESPECT
From the time of the death to the burial, the body is not left alone. A special candle is also lit and placed next to the body as a sign of respect. On the eve of the anniversary another candle is lit, known as *Yahrzeit* (meaning "year time"). The candle is left burning for 24 hours, the flame symbolizing the soul of the deceased.

Yahrzeit candle

An old Jewish cemetery in Worms, Germany

MOURNING CUSTOMS
A seven-day mourning period begins on the day of the burial. This is known as *shiva* (meaning "seven") and usually takes place at the home of the deceased. All mirrors in the house are covered, and mourners sit on low stools, reciting the *kaddish*, a prayer in praise of God and affirming life. For close family of the deceased, the mourning continues for 12 months, during which all parties and celebrations are avoided.

Shofar

High Holy Days

The themes of forgiveness and repentance are reflected in the most important holy days in Judaism—*Rosh Hashanah* (the Jewish New Year) and *Yom Kippur* (the Day of Atonement). These High Holy Days are commemorated in September or October, depending on the Hebrew calendar. Synagogues are filled to capacity, with many running overflow services for those who don't normally attend during the year. *Rosh Hashanah* is followed 10 days later by a day of prayer and fasting called *Yom Kippur*. For Jews, this entire period is a critical time when God not only decides their fate but also shows mercy to those who want to mend their ways.

Rosh Hashanah

This festival marks the creation of the world. It is also seen as a time of judgment when God balances a person's good deeds against their bad deeds, and decides what will be in store for them in the coming year. His judgment is noted in one of three books: one for the good, one for the wicked, and one for the average person. During the next 10 days, known as the Days of Awe, people are given a chance to repent, since God's final judgment is sealed at *Yom Kippur*.

THE SHOFAR
During *Rosh Hashanah*, synagogue services are longer and more solemn than usual, and include a confession and prayers of repentance. An important ritual associated with the occasion is the sounding of the *shofar*, often made from a ram's horn as a reminder of the ram that was sacrificed by Abraham. The sound of the *shofar* is also intended to be a wake-up call, inspiring people to reflect on the year that is ending and resolve to lead a better life in the coming year.

TASHLIKH
On the afternoon of *Rosh Hashanah*, some people go to a river or the sea and recite prayers. As a symbolic gesture, they empty their pockets and throw breadcrumbs into the water to represent their sins. This custom is called *tashlikh*, which means "casting away."

52

A Happy New Year!

לְשָׁנָה טוֹבָה תִכָּתֵבוּ !

תכתבו

Rosh Hashanah card

NEW YEAR CUSTOMS
In some communities, people send New Year cards. Unlike secular New Year celebrations, this is a time for Jewish people to ask forgiveness from God and from those who have been wronged.

Kiwi fruit

Papaya

Honey

Apple

A SWEET NEW YEAR
On the eve of the festival it is customary to eat a piece of apple dipped in honey in the hope that the new year will be sweet. People also eat an exotic fruit they have not eaten for some time or wear new clothes.

Tzedakah (charity) box

Yom Kippur

The holiest day of the Jewish calendar is *Yom Kippur*. Apart from the ill or those taking medicine, everyone above the age of *Bar* or *Bat Mitzvah* fasts for 25 hours, and most people spend the entire day praying in a synagogue to make amends with their creator. The *Yom Kippur* service ends with a single blast of the *shofar*, and everyone returns home feeling cleansed and with a new sense of purpose.

Jonah being cast into the sea for disobeying God

GIVING TO CHARITY
The High Holy Day prayers say that those who sincerely repent, pray, and give charity will be granted a good year. Although no money is handled on *Yom Kippur* itself, in many synagogues, the rabbi will make an appeal encouraging people to donate money to a particular charity.

THE BOOK OF JONAH
On *Yom Kippur* the Book of Jonah is read in the synagogue. It recounts the story of Jonah, who is asked by God to tell the people of Nineveh to repent. At first, Jonah refuses, but God forces him to deliver the message. The people ask for forgiveness and are saved, demonstrating God's compassion.

Festivals

THERE ARE MANY IMPORTANT religious festivals throughout the Jewish year. Some mark key events in the history of Judaism, while others have an agricultural significance. The festivals are celebrated not only in synagogues but with various rituals at home, too, each one marked with a different type of food. In addition, the Sabbath, or *Shabbat* in Hebrew, provides a weekly structure for the year. Each festival starts on the evening before the event and then continues on the next day, because in biblical times a day began at sunset, since that was a way of marking time.

THE SUKKAH
The *sukkah* is a temporary shelter. It is built with three walls and a small gap left in the roof so that people can see the stars— a reminder that God is looking after them. Although some families build a hut in their yards, some synagogues also have a communal *sukkah* for people to use after the service.

Sukkot

The week-long festival of *Sukkot* (meaning "huts") is celebrated five days after the solemn High Holy Days. *Sukkot* commemorates the time when the Israelites lived in temporary dwellings during the Exodus from Egypt, and also celebrates the gathering of the final harvest. A ritual associated with *Sukkot* is the blessing over the four plants—a palm branch, an *etrog* (citrus fruit), myrtle, and willow. These are known as the Four Species, or the *Lulav*, and represent the agriculture on which we all depend.

Etrog

Willow

Myrtle

FOUR SPECIES
During the synagogue service, the four plants are are waved in all directions. This is to show that God is everywhere.

Palm branch

Blessings are recited on the Four Species

DECORATING THE SUKKAH
It is customary for children to help decorate the *sukkah* with pictures, paper chains, and seasonal fruit, representing the autumn harvest. Meals are eaten in the huts, and sometimes people sleep there too.

THE PROCESSION
On each day of the festival a blessing is said while holding the Four Species. On the seventh day of *Sukkot*, followers end the morning service by walking seven times around the synagogue. The figure seven is symbolic of the seven processions made by the priests around the Temple during biblical times.

Simchat Torah

Immediately after *Sukkot* comes *Simchat Torah* (meaning "rejoicing over the *Torah*"). The festival marks the end of the *Torah* readings and the start of a new cycle of readings. This shows that God's words are continuous. Amid dancing and clapping, all the *Torah* scrolls are taken out of the Ark and paraded several times around the synagogue or in the streets.

A *Torah* procession at the Western Wall, Israel

Chocolate coins

HANUKKAH TRADITIONS
During *Hanukkah*, people usually eat food cooked in oil, such as *latkes* (potato pancakes) and doughnuts. This serves as a reminder of the miracle of the oil. In some communities children also receive money or chocolate coins.

Latkes

Candy is given to children in the synagogue on Simchat Torah

LIGHTING THE MENORAH
On each night of *Hanukkah*, the family gathers to recite blessings, light the candles, and sing *Hanukkah* songs. The *hanukkiya,* or *menorah,* holds eight candles as well as a servant candle to light the others. The newest candle is lit first, then the others are kindled. By the end of the week, all eight candles are lit, symbolizing the miracle of the oil in the Temple.

Hanukkah

The festival of *Hanukkah* commemorates an important historical event. Nearly 2,000 years ago, Jews in ancient Israel were not allowed to practice their faith. A monumental battle was won when they rebelled against their foreign rulers. Judah the Maccabee, leader of the revolt, rededicated the Temple, which had been used for pagan worship. The eternal lamp was relit, and although they only had enough oil to last one day, miraculously the oil lasted for eight days.

A candle is lit on each night

THE DREIDEL
While the candles burn, children play with a special spinning top called a *dreidel*. On each of its four sides is a Hebrew letter standing for the words "a great miracle happened there."

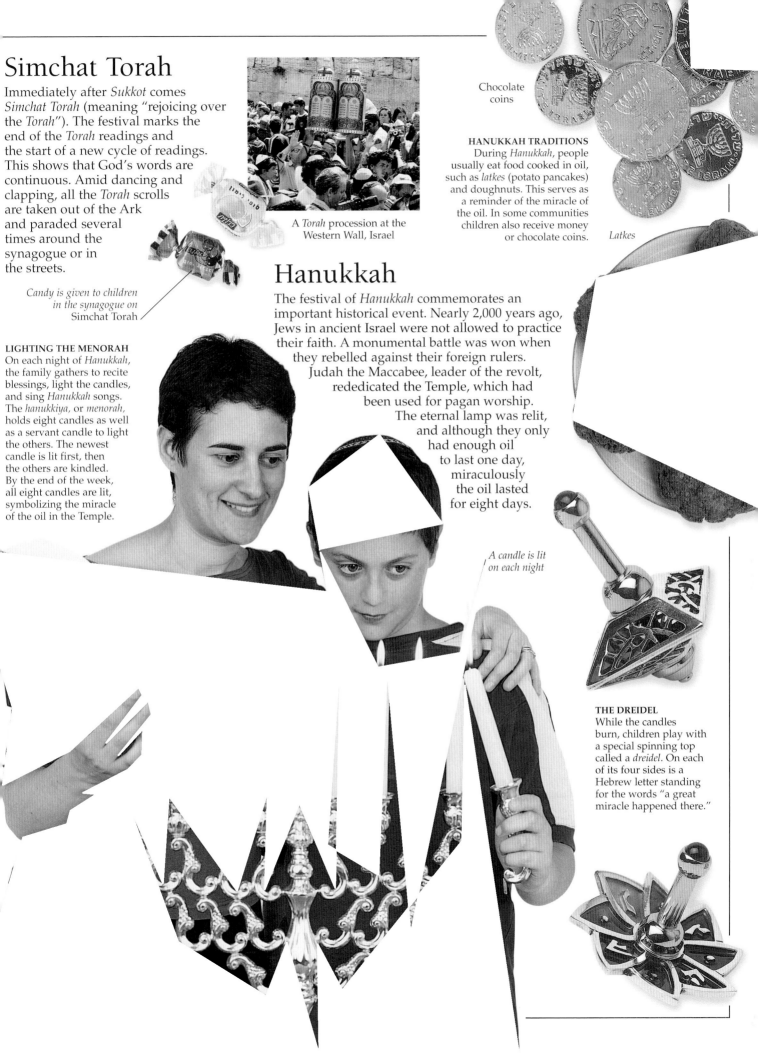

Continued from previous page

Olive branch

Tu Bishvat

The minor festival of *Tu Bishvat* is also known as the New Year for Trees. Historically, 10 percent of agricultural produce had to be given to priests and the poor on *Tu Bishvat*. In Israel today, the festival is seen as a time to plant new trees and for eating the fruits of the land.

PLANTING TREES
Some school children in Israel plant a sapling on *Tu Bishvat,* which falls in January, the start of Spring. Jews in other communities are also encouraged to sponsor a tree in Israel through the Jewish National Fund.

Gregger

THE SERVICE
The synagogue service reflects the fun spirit of *Purim.* Whenever the name of Haman is mentioned, people hiss, stamp their feet, or shake rattles, known as *greggers.*

Purim

A fun and entertaining festival, *Purim* is usually celebrated in March. The main ritual associated with *Purim* is the reading of the *Megillah* (the Book of Esther). It recounts the story of a Jewish woman called Esther and her cousin Mordecai, who lived in Persia (now Iran) in the 5th century BCE. They devised a plan to stop a villainous court official, Haman, from killing Persian Jews.

THE SCROLL
On the eve of *Purim,* and on the day itself, Jews gather in the synagogue to read the *Megillah.* Unlike other biblical books, there is no mention of God in the Book of Esther. Observant Jews believe that this shows God is always working, even in ways that are not obvious.

Esther   Mordecai

The story of Esther is handwritten on parchment

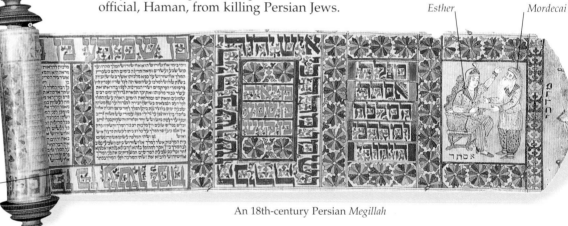

An 18th-century Persian *Megillah*

THE PARADE
As well as listening to the *Megillah,* people eat a festive meal, exchange gifts of food, and give to charity. Some Jewish communities organize parties and parades. Often children and adults wear colorful costumes to add to the festive atmosphere.

The annual *Purim* parade in Tel Aviv, Israel

Bitter
herb

An egg reminds Jews of
the sacrifices made in
biblical times

Meat symbolizes the
lamb sacrificed on
the first Passover

Bitter herbs
reflect the bitter
experience of
slavery

Green
vegetables represent
spring and new life

Charoset *(a nut and fruit paste)*
is symbolic of the mortar used
by Jewish slaves to build the cities

Passover

In March or April Jews celebrate
the important festival of Passover, or
Pesach in Hebrew. Jews commemorate
the time when the people of Israel
were led out of Egypt by Moses—this
was the beginning of a Jewish nation.
A celebratory meal, called a *seder*
(a Hebrew word meaning "order"),
takes place during the Passover.
The family gathers to eat this special
meal, recount the story of the Exodus,
and sing songs of praise to God.

THE HAGGADAH
The festival lasts for eight days, and
on the first two nights, the story of
the Exodus from Egypt is read from the
Haggadah. A child present at the meal asks
four questions from the *Haggadah*, and by
retelling the story, the questions are
answered. In the past, the *Haggadah*
was written and illustrated by hand,
and some of these have survived to the
present day. The detail of the Passover
meal shown below is from a medieval
German version.

THE PASSOVER TABLE
The *seder* plate is used only for the
Passover meal. The food on the plate
symbolizes the story of the Israelites
in ancient Egypt (c. 1290–1224 BCE).
A glass of salt water is also placed
on the table to symbolize the bitter
tears of the enslaved Israelites.

Matzos

UNLEAVENED BREAD
When the Israelites
left Egypt in a hurry,
the only food they
were able to take was
some bread that had
not risen. Today, Jews
refrain from eating
any food that
contains leaven
(yeast), known as
chametz. This includes
bread, so people eat
matzo instead. It is
also important not
to have any leavened
food in the home
during Passover.

Continued from previous page

Omer

In ancient Israel, the 49 days between Passover and the festival of *Shavuot* were counted. This period was known as the *Omer*. It marked the end of the barley harvest and the start of the wheat harvest. A sheaf (*omer* in Hebrew) from the new season's barley crop was offered at the Temple in Jerusalem.

LAG BAOMER

Day 33 of the *Omer* calendar is known as *Lag BaOmer*. A rabbi, Shimon bar Yochai, is said to have revealed mystical secrets contained in the *Kabbalah* on this day. Another tradition tells the story of Rabbi Akiva, a noted *Torah* scholar who lost 24,000 of his students in an epidemic during the *Omer* period. However, on the *Lag BaOmer*, no one died. Some people light bonfires to mark the occasion.

OMER CALENDAR

Although there is no Temple or *omer* offering today, some observant Jews still count down the days between Passover and *Shavuot*. They use a special calendar to help them keep track of the days.

Omer calendar for children

SEVEN SPECIES

As well as the commandments, *Shauvot* celebrates the bringing of the first fruits (shown below) to the Temple in Jerusalem. These fruits have always been identified with the land of Israel.

Barley

Dates

Grapes

Shavuot

The Greek name for the festival of *Shavuot* is *Pentecost*, from the word for "fifty," because it begins after the 49 days of the *Omer* period. *Shavuot* celebrates the giving of the *Torah* by God to Moses on Mount Sinai and the beginning of a new wheat harvest. During the synagogue service, the Ten Commandments and the Book of Ruth are read. The festival lasts for two days.

Wheat

Figs

Children in a kibbutz school celebrate Shavuot as a harvest festival

Olives

Pomegranates

TRADITIONS

On *Shavuot*, some people eat dairy foods. This is a reminder of the time when the Israelites ate only dairy food while waiting to hear the commandments—they wanted to avoid eating meat forbidden in the dietary laws. Synagogues are also decorated with flowers to celebrate the giving of the commandments, and very observant Jews stay up all night learning the *Torah*.

Cup for washing hands

Shabbat

The Jewish day of rest, the Sabbath is known in Hebrew as the *Shabbat*. It begins every Friday at sunset with the lighting of the *Shabbat* candles and ends the following Saturday night. In Jewish communities, the *Shabbat* is observed in various ways.

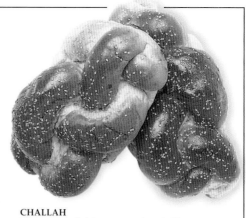

CHALLAH
The two *challah* loaves on the *Shabbat* table recall the time when the Israelites wandered in the desert. God gave them manna to eat every day, but on Friday they received double the amount.

WASHING HANDS
Before the start of *Shabbat*, some Jews wash their hands three times with a special two-handed cup. Only when this is done can the *Shabbat* meal begin.

"Remember the Sabbath day and keep it holy. On the seventh day you shall do no work."

ONE OF THE TEN COMMANDMENTS

Shabbat table

Havdalah candle

HAVDALAH
The ceremony marking the end of *Shabbat* is called *havdalah*, which means "separation." It features a braided candle, wine, and sweet-smelling spices. *Havdalah* emphasizes the separation between the holy *Shabbat* and the other days of the week.

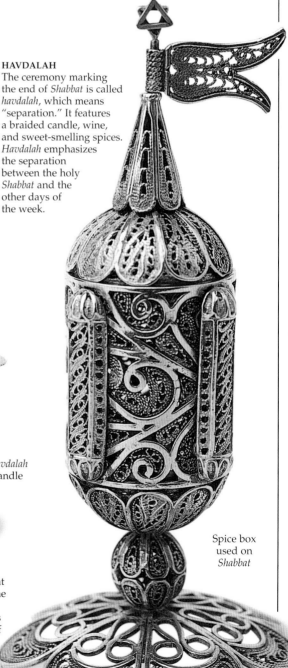

Spice box used on *Shabbat*

THE MEANING OF SHABBAT
Just as God rested on the seventh day after creating the world, observant Jews do not work at all on *Shabbat*. It is traditional to invite guests home for the *Shabbat* evening meal, especially those without families. Essentially, *Shabbat* is seen as a time to worship, rest, and be with the community.

BRAIDED CANDLE
The *havdalah* candle brings to mind the light created by God when he brought order to the world. Its many wicks symbolize the unity of the Jewish people.

Jewish contribution

Despite the prejudice that existed against the Jewish people—which lasted well into the 20th century and beyond—their contribution to all aspects of life has been remarkable. Always driven by the desire to excel and inspire, both intellectually and academically, the Jewish people have felt motivated to make their mark—from the lasting legacy of music and painting to pioneering breakthroughs in science and medicine and cutting-edge technology to improve people's lives. The prejudice and hostility faced by Jews over the years, however, has often been incorporated into the emotion of their work, whether a painting, a novel, or the desire to negotiate a more tolerant and peaceful world.

The arts

From pianist to poet and author to artist, Jews have enriched the world through their passion for music, painting, literature, and design. A combination of drive and imagination, bravado and brilliance have kept them at the forefront of everything that is exciting in the arts. It was immigrants to the US who, almost single-handedly, set up the early studios in Hollywood—including Metro-Goldwyn-Mayer (MGM), 20th Century Fox, and Warner Brothers.

DESIGN
Arne Jacobsen (1902–71), a Danish architect, achieved fame in 1958 with his modern SAS Hotel in Copenhagen, constructed using tinted glass. This revolutionary design influenced architects the world over. During World War II, however, Jacobsen had to leave Denmark for Sweden, but returned after the war. His 1950s and 1960s furniture designs, such as the egg chair, are still selling today.

PAINTING
Marc Chagall (1887–1985) was born into a devoutly Jewish family in Russia, where he was first exposed to anti-Semitism. In 1910, he moved to Paris, France, to further his career as an artist, but left for the US following German occupation. His life in Russia, together with the experiences of World War II and the revelation of the death camps, had a profound impact on his work.

MUSIC
One of the greatest violin virtuosos, Yehudi Menuhin (1916–99) impressed audiences from the age of seven, when he performed with the San Francisco Symphony Orchestra. He was world-famous for his technical ability and sensitive interpretation.

LITERATURE OF THE MIND
Sigmund Freud (1856–1939) studied medicine in Austria, and went on to develop a new science of the mind—psychoanalysis. He popularized his ideas in books such as *The Interpretation of Dreams*. Freud left Austria for England in 1938 to escape the Nazi occupation.

The egg chair

Community by Marc Chagall

Film poster for *Schindler's List* (1995)

FILMMAKING

After success with films such as *Jaws* and *ET*, director Steven Spielberg gave millions of people their first insight into the Holocaust with *Schindler's List*. As part of the filmmaking process, Spielberg recorded the memories of more than 50,000 Holocaust survivors.

Politics

A history of a people in turmoil, together with the Jewish teaching that demands concern for less fortunate people, has led many Jews to become involved in politics. The ideal of a tolerant people living in a peaceful world continues to be a driving force at both local and national levels.

President Bill Clinton witnesses the historic handshake outside the White House, Washington, DC, in September 1993

Yitzhak Rabin

PEACEMAKERS

After heading the armed forces in the Six-Day War, Yitzhak Rabin (1922–95) became Ambassador to the US. In 1992, as Prime Minister of Israel, he put the Israeli–Arab peace process on his political agenda and, in 1995, won the Nobel Peace Prize. However, some people opposed his ideas, and he was assassinated at a peace rally in Tel Aviv, Israel.

DIPLOMACY

Henry Kissinger (b. 1923) was a refugee from Nazi Germany who went on to teach at Harvard University. He later became US Secretary of State. In 1972, he organized President Nixon's historic visits to Russia and China. The following year Kissinger was awarded the Nobel Peace Prize.

Yasser Arafat, joint winner of the Nobel Peace Prize

The pioneers

Everything from the clothes we wear to the way we travel has been influenced by Jewish pioneers. Often facing prejudice in established industries, Jews preferred to work in new fields, where they could use their talent to the full. They have been at the forefront of developing the technologies that have improved the lives of millions of people.

Levi's denim jeans

AVIATION DESIGN
Emile Berliner (1851–1929) was the grandson of a rabbi who emigrated from Germany to the US. A prolific inventor and experimenter, in 1919 he developed a prototype helicopter.

CLOTHES DESIGN
The blue jeans worn everywhere today were invented by Levi Strauss (1829–1902). Born in Germany, Strauss moved to California, where gold had been discovered. While selling tent canvas to miners, he heard them complain that their trousers wore out too quickly. He made them blue jeans with rivets on the pockets—and the hard-wearing item became a global success.

Helena Rubenstein highlights the basic contours of the face

BEAUTY SPECIALIST
Helena Rubenstein (1870–1965) revolutionized the beauty industry with her waterproof mascara and medicated face creams. Born in Poland in 1871, she built up a beauty empire in Australia, Europe, and the US. In 1953, she created the Helena Rubenstein Foundation, which cared for needy women and children.

The classic Olivetti M-40 typewriter

OFFICE TECHNOLOGY
Italian activist Adriano Olivetti (1901–60) built his father's typewriter company into the largest manufacturer of business machines in Europe. Wanted by the Gestapo during World War II, Adriano and his father went into hiding, while their factory became headquarters for the resistance movement.

INDUSTRIAL ENGINEERING
The son of a gem merchant from Poland, French industrialist André Citroën (1878–1935) was a marketing man who understood his public. He designed a range of affordable cars for the French working man. Citroën even had his name in lights on the Eiffel Tower to promote his cars.

381-HC 92

Citroën
Traction Avant

Henry Berliner, Emile's son, makes a test flight in the new American "chopper"

Berliner's flying machine had a rotating blade that would lift it straight up into the air

Science and medicine

The Jewish contribution to the understanding of science and to breakthroughs in medical care has been monumental. Without the dedication of physicists and chemists, much of our knowledge of the world might still be a mystery. In medicine, Jews have been responsible for discovering vaccines to combat many killer diseases, including cholera, bubonic plague, typhoid fever, and polio.

PHYSICS
One of the world's greatest scientists, Albert Einstein (1879–1955) formulated the theory of relativity, which changed the way people viewed the world. In 1921, he was awarded the Nobel Prize for Physics. Born in Germany, Einstein moved to Switzerland as a young man. He taught in Europe, but when the Nazis came to power, he settled in the US. Einstein's insights into the nature of matter made the atomic bomb a reality—something he always regretted.

Paul Ehrlich, bacteriologist, at work in his laboratory

MEDICAL SCIENCE
Paul Ehrlich (1854–1915) was born in Germany. He developed the idea of the "magic bullet"—a drug that would only attack the diseased parts of the body without damaging healthy cells and tissues. This work earned him the Nobel Prize for Medicine in 1908.

Cluster of polio viruses

THE FIGHT TO CURE POLIO
The first polio vaccine—to fight the disease that killed thousands—was developed by US virologist Jonas Salk (1914–45). His vaccine was administered by injection. However, it was Polish American Albert Sabin (1906–93) who developed the oral vaccine that was approved for worldwide use. Sabin's objective, to wipe out the disease by the year 2000, was eventually achieved.

Index

Acknowledgements

Dorling Kindersley would like to thank:
Steimatzky and Jerusalem the Golden for their generosity
Design assistance: Sheila Collins
Editorial assistance: Fran Jones, Sadie Smith, Clare Lister, and Zahavit Shalev **Index:** Hilary Bird

The publisher would like to thank the following for their kind permission to reproduce their photographs:
a-above; b-below; c-center; l-left; r-right; t-top

AKG London: 9tl, 15c, 18c, 26b, 27tr, 29tc, 41cbr; Erich Lessing 58tr; Stefan Diller 19l. **Ancient Art & Architecture Collection:** 14cr, 16b, 40bl. **Arcaid:** Alan Weintraub 33cl. **The Art Archive:** Biblioteca Nacional Lisbon/Dagli Orti 53br; Bibliotheque des Arts Decoratifs Paris/Dagli Orti 9cb; Dagli Orti 10cl; Israel Museum Jerusalem/Dagli Orti 1c; Museuo Capitolino Rome/Dagli Orti 17br; Nationalmuseet Copenhagen Denmark/Dagli Orti (A) 19br.

Art Directors & TRIP: Ask Images 48tr; H Rogers 39tl, 47br; I. Genut 40c; S. Shaprio 54tr. **Art Resource:** The Jewish Museum, New York 56c. **Rabbi Eliezer Ben-Yehuda:** 47tl. **Werner Braun:** 52br, 55tc, 56b. **Bridgeman Art Library, London/New York:** Basilica di San Marco, Venice, Italy 8tr; Bibliotheque Nationale, Paris 12bl; Bibliotheque Nationale, Paris, France 18br; British Library, London 13c; Giraudon 38tl; Lauros/Giraudon 57br; Musee de la Revolution Francaise, Vizille, France 21tl; Private Collection 20cr, 39br. **British Library:** 47tr. **British Museum:** 8cl, 8c. **Camera Press:** 29cb, 29br. **Citroën UK Ltd:** 62b. **Coca-Cola Company:** 47bl. **Corbis:** 60br; Araldo de Luca 62cr; Archivo Iconografico, S.A 6tl, 6cr, 15tr; Barry Lewis 32bl; Bettmann 22bl, 28c, 28bl, 31cl, 62-63tc, 63cl, 63b; Burstein Collection 60-61tc; Dean Conger 8-9b, 11tr; Gianni Dagli Orti 10b, 14tl; Hayan Isachar 54b; Leonard de Selva 24cl; Moshe Shai 58tl; Nathan Benn 17tl; Paul A. Souders 34br; Peter M. Wilson 38bl; Peter Turnley 46bl;

Rabbi Naamah Kelman 44c; Richard T. Nowitz 6b, 14b, 32tr, 58br; Shai Ginott 46br; Stapleton Collection 36tr; Ted Spiegel 31bc; Unger Kevin/Sygma 45cra; West Semitic Research/Dead Sea Scrolls Foundation 37tc. **E & E Picture Library:** 59b. **Mary Evans Picture Library:** 12tl, 18tl, 24bl, 26tl, 26c, 27tl, 27cl, 53tl; Cassell, Petter & Galpin 22tr; Explorer Archives 40tl; Weimar Archive 31tr. **Moshe Frumin:** 12br. **Glasgow Museum:** 2c, 4bcl, 52tl. **Golders Green United Synagogue:** 4l, 54l. **Ronald Grant Archive:** 21b. **Sonia Halliday Photographs:** 8br, 9c, 13cr. **Fritz Hansen A/S:** 60bl. **Robert Harding Picture Library:** E. Simanor 43b; M. F. Chillmaid 19tr. **Beth Hatefutsoth, Photo Archive, Tel Aviv:** 18bl; 25t, 32cr, 44tl; Central Zionist Archives, Jerusalem 22cl, 24tr, 25br, 25c; Courtesy of E. M. Stern 45cb; Ghetto Fighter's House-Photo Archive 30c; Jewish National and University Library, Jerusalem 39tr; Municipal Archives of Rome 20tr; Tel Aviv, The Gross Family Collection 24br. **Heritage Image Partnership:** British Museum 13tr; The British Museum 14cl. © **Michael Holford:** 9r. **Hulton Archive/Getty Images:** 22-23bc, 23cr,

26tr, 27br, 29tl, 29cr, 30bl, 62cl; Leo Baeck Inst. NYC. Photo Gemeinden Deutschland. Macdonald and Co. 27cb. **Hutchison Library:** J. Horner 42cr. **Impact Photos:** Stewart Weir 47bcr. **Imperial War Museum:** 28tl, 28br; James Johnson 30tl, 30cla. **Israelimages.com:** Avi Hirschfield 7bl; Israel Talby 32br, 45t; Richard Nowitz 46cb. **Israel Museum Jerusalem:** 11l, 16tl, 38-39bc, 48bl; D. Harris 48c; David Harris 51tr, 51cl. **Oscar Israelowitz:** 33tr. **Jewish Education Bureau:** 50cla. **Jewish Museum, London:** 2cr, 3c, 5tr, 16cl, 40-41cbl, 50tl. **Joods Historisch Museum:** 20bl. **Kobal Collection:** 61tr. **Levi Strauss & Co:** 62tl. **Christine Osborne:** 56c. **Popperfoto:** REUTERS 61bc. **Zev Radovan, Jerusalem:** 11cl, 11br, 12tr, 13cl, 15tl, 15tc, 15br, 16c, 17bl, 17r, 20tl, 37cl, 37br, 44bl, 44-45bc, 45br, 49tr, 49b, 50bc, 54cr. **Rex Features:** London Weekend 60bc; SIPA Press 61bl. **Anat Rotem, Jerusalem:** 7t. **Science Photo Library:** CDC 63cr. **Topham Picturepoint:** 29bc. **JerryYoung:** 42bl.

All other images © Dorling Kindersley. For further information see: www.dkimages.com